YOUR TIME FOR CHANGE

HOW TO BE THE BEST YOU CAN BECOME

Part I

Dudley Wolford

Copyright© 1999 by Dudley Wolford

Other books by the author:

You Can Make It Happen!
Two Moves To Better Golf

Published by BRENTWOOD PRODUCTIONS
P.O. Box 1780
SISTERS, OR 97759
(541) 549-2014

Printed by MAVERICK PUBLICATIONS, INC.
63324 Nels Anderson Rd.
Bend, OR 97701
(541) 382-6978

Printed in the United States of America
Library of Congress Card Number: 99-094534
ISBN 1-882091-03-5

TABLE OF CONTENTS

All human misery is the result of ignorance; and nothing but knowledge of *self* can overcome it.

Dudley Wolford

AUTHOR'S NOTE

At the outset I would just like to say, that whatever it is you're looking for in life, you're going to find the answers here. I say this with confidence, because you are about to come to know yourself for *who* and *what* you truly are. And in terms of the human experience, this is essential if you ever expect to make things happen in your life as you want them to be ...increase your income, lower your golf handicap, improve your self-esteem, increase sales, lose excessive weight, eliminate unwanted habits, and so on.

As you will find, much of what you will be reading here is based upon material dating back to the time when man first asked himself, "Who am I?" Parts of it will have a familiar ring, and some will not. Yet, in the over-all picture, each piece put in its proper place, you will find it meaningful and very much worthwhile in terms of understanding, both yourself and others, and learning how to cope with your surroundings successfully.

Because of the nature of the material presented in the beginning, there is a possibility you might question its relevance as it pertains to your immediate needs in self-improvement. If you should, let me say this: There is absolutely nothing associated with the human experience which is not relevant insofar as self-insight is concerned. It was Socrates who so profoundly and concisely expressed this when he said: *Anyone who truly knows himself will succeed, for he will know, precisely wherein his capabilities lie and the area in which to apply them; whereas anyone who doesn't know himself, he will frequently blunder, even to the point of ruining his life.*

Frankly, it took me a lot of years to figure out just what the old boy meant. For sure, he wasn't referring to knowing one's name. What he was suggesting was, that a man *who* truly knows himself understands himself completely, from every aspect ...his potential and capability, *why* he thinks

i

and behaves as he does, and *what* he can do to change the conditions in his life as he wants them to be ...all of which is a far cry from what most of us think we know about ourselves today.

Hopefully you will view what is written here with an open mind. It will surely be one of the most rewarding experiences of your life. And if you will allow it, the knowledge and insight you should gain from this brief study will literally change your life for the better.

As you will soon discover, it is solely because of what *you* chose to think yesterday that you find yourself as you are today. Once you learn how to think in terms of the way you want things to be today, so you will find them to be in your life tomorrow.

THE REASON WHY

If I were to ask any one of you who were born in the 50s how you feel about the state of our society today compared to how it was forty years ago, you probably wouldn't notice much of a change. But for those of us born in the 20s, we've certainly seen a dramatic change. Mostly bad. For example, shortly after WWII our country was the most envied nation in the world. A chance for anyone to live the American dream was very much alive. We had the highest standard of living of any society in the world. It took only one bread winner's income to live a comfortably life. There was very little sexual promiscuity, use of drugs, crime, violence or government intrusion in our lives. Today it's a different story. In most cases it takes two incomes just to break even because our workers are making substantially less in real dollars than they did twenty to thirty years ago. Many of our public schools subject their students to body search and metal detectors in order to gain entrance to class rooms. Some of our senior citizens are eating dog food just to survive. Homelessness, something that didn't exist before, is a growing trend on a grand scale, as are the number of youths and adults who are hopelessly getting hooked on drugs.

Crime, rape, violence, and child abuse is out of hand. The same is true of our family values, what's being taught or not taught in public education, and what's being viewed in the mass media and television. And then there are those of us who don't quite fit into the category of the afore-mentioned, but who, never-the-less, have a variety of personal problems, but not so depressing. The bottom line is that as individuals and as a nation, we are confused and frustrated looking for answers. Other than band-aids handed down from Washington, little has been done to turn things around, meaning more of the same until it's too late.

So how do we turn this tide of degradation that has overtaken us, both as individuals and as a nation? The first thing is to determine what's involved; who's doing the suffering and what's the cause of it? Obviously it is the likes of the lesser well-off who are doing the suffering. As for what's causing it? this age-old question has been asked before in history: It was Pogo who came up with the answer: *We have met the enemy, and he is us.* And of course he was right. We've got a people problem all right, and we're the cause of it; we're the cause of it because of our innocence of ignorance; our ignorance of self in terms of who we really are, why we are what we are at any moment in lives, and more importantly, what each of us can do to make things happen in our lives just as we want them to be ...to be the best we can become. That's our real problem! As a society, we know all about taking out our frustrations on others. But we don't know the first thing about ourselves, or why we do what we do. Just as Socrates said: "...*anyone who doesn't know himself, (he) will frequently blunder, even to the point of ruining his life* ...something far too many of us have been doing for too long.

So what are we going to do about it? Well, as the title suggests, it's YOUR TIME FOR CHANGE! It's time to overcome your innocence of ignorance through enlightenment. It's time to be presented with the facts, the truths and the scientifically proven principles as they apply to the human experience, the consequence of which will provide you with all the ingredients necessary to make your life more meaningful and purposeful in the days ahead.

Possibly for the first time in your life you are going to have the opportunity of seeing yourself for *who* and *what* you truly are. You're going to come to an understanding of wherein your potential and capabilities lie; you're going to come to an understanding of how your mental system operates; your going to know *why* you think the thoughts you do and consequently affect your system's actions; and you're going to come to an understanding of *how* your mental system can be programmed with thoughts of your own choosing and in turn cause you to respond accordingly.

iv

In short, what you will be learning here is analogous to being given the keys to the proverbial candy store, making it possible for you to feast upon doing or becoming anything you desire: making more money, enjoying better health, excelling in sports and skills, developing a better personality, breaking unwanted habits, being more creative, or whatever. It makes no difference as to what it is you want. Once you have gained a true insight of yourself, as presented here, you, the maker of yourself and your circumstances, will come to the realization that there is nothing you cannot do or accomplish because you already possess all the potential and capability needed to make things happen in your life ...just as you want them to be! All that's needed is to be informed that such is the case.

My most fervent hope is that after you have had a chance to absorb what's to be presented here and the opportunity to personally experience its benefits, that you will pass what you've learned on to others ...your wife or husband, your friends, your children, your grandchildren, whom ever, because possessing a true insight of self is the only solution to over-coming the degrading ignorance we have allowed to creep into our lives and our nation. And it is only when enough people come to this realization, that we, individually and collectively, will be able to rid ourselves of its consequences and get on with our lives ...in pursuit of the American dream.

Let us begin.

BORN TO WIN

If you would understand anything, observe its beginnings and its development.

Aristotle

Long ago it was written: ...in the beginning the earth was without form and void ...darkness was upon the face of the deep ...the Spirit of God was moving on the face of the waters ...God said: Let there be light ...there was light ...God said: Let the waters bring forth abundantly to moving creatures that have life and fowl that may fly above the earth in the open expanse of the heaven ...God created man in his own image ...the image of God created he him; male and female he created them.

To many of us, this six-thousand year-old bit of biblical account of creation is regarded as historical fact. In the seventeenth century, one in particular who accepted this account as fact, an Irish archbishop, calculated the date of the creation by studying genealogies recorded in the Bible. His conclusion was that God made the world in 4004 B.C.

Two hundred years later, a number of Naturalists of 19th century England had some questions for God, such as: Why did He make so many species? Why should there be thousands of kinds of birds? "And why, for heaven's sakes, should there be over a million kinds of bugs? And why, God, did you bury the bones of unknown animals in ancient rocks? "And why did you make so many high mountains look like they were once at the bottom of the sea, even to the point of garnishing them with countless layers of sea shells?

As most school children know today through the efforts of scientific exploration and analysis ...in particular those conducted by the physical and biological sciences, most of these questions have been pretty well answered, including how planet Earth evolved as well as the living things that inhabit it. Much of the credit responsible for providing us with this knowledge lies with concepts and research put forth by a divinity student drop-out of Cambridge University, a born Naturalist, Charles Darwin. What Darwin gave the world was a scientific explanation of why and how all living things on planet Earth came to exist as they do today. Based upon his theory of Natural Selection, he visualized the progress of biological evolution as being like that of a tree. From a solid trunk representing a very limited number of primitive organisms, over time, sprouted the stout branches of fish and reptiles and plants and insects and mammals. They, in turn, branched out again and again until finally there were branches representing roses and radishes, pigeons and peacocks, monkeys, apes, and humans.

Darwin theorized, that in the random shuffle of heredity, each new individual organism is born slightly different from others. Occasionally an individual will be born who is stronger, faster, or better able to cope with a changing world. That individual will thrive and pass on the advantage to its offspring. Generation upon generation of small naturally selected changes accumulate until the new organism no longer breeds what its ancestor had been, at which time a new species has evolved. Thus, long random survival, over countless generations, leads to a gradual evolutionary change. From small beginnings on our planet, such as a single cell or bacteria, over a sufficiently large number of these long randomly selected generations, Nature comes up with highly complex designed species; mammals, birds, and creatures like you and me.

When Darwin published his theory of natural selection in 1859 (Origin of Species), as predictable, it brought about a shocking response from the angelical public, in that it indirectly refuted the accepted (at the time) creation theory depicted in the Bible. Today, through observation and greater scientific understanding, we now know his theory to be scientifically correct. From an "observable" aspect, one needs only to witness a race between a thoroughbred horse and a barnyard variety. The speed and stamina of today's thoroughbred is not found in the wild. It has been created by generations upon generations of *artificial* selection ...a process in which desirable characteristics are picked out and emphasized through controlled breeding. The same can be said of not only the many "showy" flowers and high-yield plants, but also a huge variety of animal breeds from "toy" dogs to beef cattle. On the other hand, when comparing the Knights of the Round Table who were rather small ...in the 5 foot plus range... with our 7 foot plus professional basketball players... we're talking *natural* selection.

As for the "greater scientific understanding" aspect of the correctness of Darwin's theory, three Nobel Prize winners in physiology and medicine, James Watson, Francis Crick and Maurice Fredrick, gave the world a practical working model of the molecular structure of DNA (the substance that transmits the genetic information needed to creating any sort of living thing). From the model, scientist now better understand the mechanisms of inheritance, and have, subsequently, developed entirely new ways to change an organism's molecular structure through a process known as "genetic engineering." What's extraordinary about genetic engineering is that it does not work only with members of the same species, or even ones that are closely related. Instead, it allows sections of DNA to be transferred between widely different organisms and create new life forms, modify existing ones, or to produce useful biological chemicals. Today the cloning of sheep is a matter of fact. Tomorrow it will be a human being.

In that 47% of the American population doesn't believe in evolution is a frightening statistic; frightening from an educator's viewpoint, because it denies the basic unifying principle of biology, in that nothing in biology, as we know it today, makes sense except from an *evolutionary* perspective. As for those of you who may be offended by the fact that man evolved, rather than created in finished form much as he exists today, it should be pointed out that Darwin did not deny the *existence* of God, nor that God did not create man. He, Darwin, just disagreed with the Biblical account of *how* man came to be ...and I might add, so do I.

IN THE BEGINNING

According to the scientific community, the belief is that our universe came into being about 15 billion years ago as a result of a mighty explosion commonly referred to as the "big bang." Following this blast, the force of the explosion caused the universe to expand. In doing so the heat caused by the explosion began to cool and the energy generated by the heat began condensing into matter consisting mainly of hydrogen atoms. As the expansion continued further, the hydrogen atoms, in turn, tended to accumulate into vast clouds, some of which formed into galaxies. Within these galactic clouds kindled by the energy contained in the hydrogen matter, the first generation of stars were born.

At that point in time there were no planets. But deep inside the stars, nuclear fusion was creating the heavier atoms of carbon, oxygen, silicon and iron. These elements, the ash left over by the cooked hydrogen, became the raw materials from which planets and life later formed.

For a while these heavier elements were trapped in the heart of the early stars. But in the course of some of them becoming too massive, they exhausted their fuel and died. In doing so, they returned most of their substances back into space, thus enriching the local interstellar gas with the heavy elements created.

In our galaxy, the Milky Way, much of the heavy-element-enriched interstellar gas was recycled into new generations of stars and great giant turbulent clouds. In the depths of these clouds, the heavier atoms condensed into grains of rocky ice, dust and complex carbon-based molecules. And depending upon their positioning in relation to the newer generation of stars, tiny condensations of matter from these heavily enriched clouds began accreting into inconspicuous clumps of rock, metal, ice and gas that eventually became planets. Such was how science believes our solar system came into being. And such is how Earth came to be a planet, enriched with complex carbon-based molecules ...the stuff that was later to give rise to "life" as we know it today.

After Earth became a planet (some 4.5 billion years ago) its surface was inundated with water. Later, as the water subsided it left the planet with dry land and oceans. As a result of lightening and ultraviolet rays, the simple hydrogen-rich molecules of the primitive atmosphere were broken down and in turn spontaneously recombined into more and more complex molecules that later dissolved into primal soups from which the first stuff of life is thought to have originated. Then, as the soups gradually increased in complexity, a molecule arose that was able to duplicate itself, heralding the beginning of the earliest ancestor to what we now know as deoxyribonucleic acid ...DNA for short... which, as it turns out, is the master molecule of all life on earth.

BIOCHEMICAL EVOLUTION

The first living cell ...a colony of chemical molecules specializing in different functions (as defined by their respective DNA instruction)... is thought to have evolved about 4 billion years ago in the form of a plant. A billion years later a number of these single cell plants are thought to have joined together into the first multicellular organism.

About 2 billion years ago, sex evolved. And with it came a rapid change in evolution in terms of new varieties of organisms.

By 1 billion years ago, a dramatic change came over the Earth; plants, working cooperatively, started producing molecular oxygen and releasing it into the atmosphere, bringing about the demise of hydrogen-dependent organisms. Before long the Earth's atmosphere became almost totally biologically oriented, much as it is today. With this change came the Cambrian explosion, a time when a proliferation of new life forms began to break up an almost stagnant monopolization of the ponds and oceans by blue-green algae plants. From this point on evolution moved into high gear.

After the Cambrian explosion the first fish and vertebrates began appearing in rapid succession. Plants moved from the oceans and began colonizing the land. Insects evolved. Amphibians adapted to both land and water. Trees and reptiles came into being, followed by dinosaurs. Mammals emerged, followed by birds, flowers, cetaceans and primates. Less than 10 million years ago the first creature who closely resembled man arrived on the scene accompanied by a spectacular increase in brain size.

The story of real man, however, didn't begin until around five million years ago. It began with a particular type of ape-like creature on the plains of Africa, a creature referred to as Australopithecus. Such a creature was about the size of a chimpanzee. He was a descendant of the forest-living ape that lived widespread throughout Africa, Europe and Asia some ten million years ago. His hands and feet resembled those of tree-living ancestors. His limbs were not particularly well suited for running. His eye sight was well developed. By contrast, his sense of smell was poor. His teeth were not suited for grinding leaves and twigs. He most likely gathered roots, nuts, berries and fruit for food.

Evidence indicates our ape-man ancestor fashioned stone tools. He also became a hunter.

For the next 3 million years, the body of our ape man became better adapted to plains-living life. His hands developed a powerful grip. His feet became more suited to running. His spine developed a slight curve to better support the upper body. More importantly, his skull changed, allowing the jaw to become smaller and the forehead more domed. His brain doubled in size. And he grew to a height of some four and one-half feet. Today we refer to this ancestor as Homo erectus, Upright man.

Over the next million years, Upright man became more and more proficient in the making of tools and hunting prowess. He learned to use fire. He became talented in communicating. His numbers increased and began to spread into the Nile valley and northward to Europe, to the eastern shores of the Mediterranean, to Italy, the Balkans, to Java and China.

About 600,000 years ago the climate changed. Ice sheets advanced down from the north creating land bridges making it possible for migration into the Americas and the island chains of Indonesia, New Guinea and Australia.

Having evolved in the warmth of the African Savannas and feeling the intense cold of Europe, Upright man did not retreat or die out as doubtlessly most other creatures did. Instead, being dexterous of body and inventive mind, he created bone needles to sew the skins of furred animals into clothing. He made his shelter in caves, leaving artistic records on the walls and ceilings.

The last Ice Age ended about 12,000 years ago. With it came a dramatic change in the foraging and hunting life of our most recent ancestor, Homo sapien man (wise man), who gave up his nomad existence for that of village life. In the burst of new vegetation after the end of the Ice Age, a hybrid wheat appeared on the scene. Man discovered it and turned to cultivating and planting crops. He domesticated animals, built shelters, formed communities, and found a home in farming and husbandry.

Out of his settled agriculture grew the need for technology. And as before, due to his large brain and inventiveness associated with it, he responded by inventing the wheel. The rest you know as recent history. Nothing has really changed. Humankind is still evolving and inventing out of necessity in order to meet its changing needs.

Such are the highlights of your evolvement as a human being. Now let's turn to the specifics.

BIOLOGICAL EVOLUTION

At the moment ...solely by virtue of our genetic make-up... you and I belong to a species known as man. Some million years ago man's genes were associated with a species known as Lemurs, and before that they were associated with a species known as blue-green algae. How did our genetic package make the transition from algae to what it is today? Simply because of a process known as biological evolution. Biological evolution refers to the gradual process in which a chemical entity develops especially into a more complex form, a process brought about by the conditions of *time, change* and *selection.*

Time, you already know. As for the condition of *change,* we're talking about the kind of change associated with a mutation or variation in characteristics differing from its original. Such change in any organism's characteristics is generally brought about as a result of one or more of its chemical compounds of a DNA molecule ...a gene... not being copied true to the next generation, due mainly to the affects of X-rays destroying or rearranging parts of the nucleotide's chemical composition, or by an overabundance or lack of certain chemicals and/or the presence of a foreign substance that interacts unfavorably with the chemistry of the DNA molecule.

The condition of *selection*, on the other hand is associated with the *surviving* mutation or variation of what time and change has created. You see, when sex evolved some 2-billion years ago, it set the stage for two independent organisms or colony of cells to exchange their respective random mutations or variations of characteristics with one another, thus bringing a rapid multitude of new and different genetic possibilities into play for the evolvement of a far greater number of variants than were possible before sex. As we know from paleontogical history, many of the variants created by time and change in the past led to a dead end whereupon they died or became extinct; only those that withstood the test of "survival of the fittest" evolved further. A prime example of how this natural form of selection took place was outlined by Charles Darwin's discoveries in the early 1800s.

When Darwin arrived at the Galapagos Islands off the coast of Chili, he was fascinated to discover that the Galapagos animals, although similar to those found on the mainland of South America, differed in many respects from one another. The Galapagos tortoises, for instance, were much larger than those on the mainland; they even varied from island to island. In particular, Darwin noticed that tortoises who lived on a relatively well watered island ...where there was adequate ground vegetation... had short necks and a gentle curving edge to their shells just above the neck, whereas those who lived on an arid island, where the food supply was relatively scarce and mainly above ground level, had longer necks and a definite high peak in the edge of their shells to allow them to stretch their necks almost vertically. Noting a similar difference to exist among the other species of animals in the islands, Darwin came to suspect that species, per se, were not fixed forever; that in the case of the tortoises he had seen, long necks versus short necks did not evolve as separate entities, but did so due to some *natural* phenomena, a phenomena he chose to call *natural selection* ...a case of the survival of the fittest. His reasoning was as follows: In light of time and the possibility of mutations (change), all offsprings of the same species are not *identically* the same. There is a possibility, for example, that in one clutch of tortoise eggs that one of the hatchlings (due to possible minute mutant change in DNA arrangement) could be born with a longer neck than its brothers or sisters. And in the event of a drought (when the food at the ground level was scarce) the hatchling with the longer neck would stand a better chance for survival than those with shorter necks. Assuming this to be the case, and with the drought persisting, it would be quite logical, then, to assume that were the surviving hatchling allowed to mature and successfully mate and reproduce, after an extended period of time the presence of long necked tortoises would become the rule rather than the exception on an arid island where the food supply was mainly above ground level. Needless to say, Darwin's suspicions proved correct, especially in light of what the science of genetics later revealed through the works of George Mendel, Thomas Morgan, Harmann Muller, James Watson and Francis Crick.

Today there can be no doubt that all living things on earth are interrelated; that evolution and variety of species is directly related to the elements of time, change and selection. Logically, if time, change, and selection is responsible for the biological (the study of living organisms) evolution of man, it follows, then, that it must also be equally responsible for the psycho-biological (the study of mental and behavioral characteristics of living things) evolution of man since neither form of biology could exist without the presence of the other. In other words, just as there is a biological explanation for our existence, so there must be a psycho-biological explanation for why we think and behave as we do. And so there is.

PSYCHO-BIOLOGY

Much of the evidence supporting our ideas on evolution come from observations pertaining to the development of living things; a case of observing the stages through which groups of animals, including man, have passed through during the history of life on earth. For example, data taken from fossils have shown that mammals represent the latest stage in a long evolutionary series of development. Such a series began with small sea-dwelling creatures which had gristly rods instead of a backbone. Today each developing unborn mammal goes through the same evolutionary steps, in that it first develops the same gristly rod which evolves into a backbone of cartilage and in turn, evolves into bone. The same mammalian embryo develops gills, like a fish, loses them, and replaces them with lungs. Such is also true of the embryo's heart: it develops through fish, amphibian, and reptilian stages until it becomes a mammalian heart.

Like all of Nature's wonders, the brain, too, has had to travel the same road of evolution in order to develop from its humblest of beginnings to what it is today. In the sense that the great cities of the world developed from a small center and slowly grew and changed while the older parts remained intact, so it has been with the brain. Even though it has grown and developed in complexity, its older parts have remained intact because they were foundationally essential to the overall brain system. And were you to physically view any human brain from within, you'd find its present day structure reveals the stages it has passed through during its evolutionary development. Essentially, it has evolved from the inside out in three successive stages.

Starting from deep inside the brain we find the oldest part, the evolutionary core, known as the brain stem, more specifically, the Medulla Oblongata. Within this complex is the location of the neural mechanisms responsible for the basic involuntary rhythms of life ...heartbeat, blood pressure, respiration, glandular secretions, swallowing, vomiting, self-preservation and preservation of the species such as hunting, homing, mating, establishment of territory, and fighting. It is this part of the brain that is associated with our *reptilian* ancestry.

From here the brain evolved to the next stage; the Cerebellum, the part of the brain associated with our *mammalian* ancestry, which is the major source of our moods and emotions, of our concern and care for our young, grooving a golf swing, guiding the hand holding a wine glass to the mouth without spilling the contents, threading a needle, and so on.

Capping out the third stage of the brain's development is the Cerebrum, the highest order of brain development to date. Working in conjunction with the other two older brains in the struggle for survival, the cerebrum is where much of the electro-biochemical communication taking place in the brain is transformed into consciousness awareness; the realm of our intuition and critical analysis. Accounting for more than two-thirds of the brain's mass, the Cerebrum accounts for our most human qualities ...imagination, language, the ability to reason, to deal with symbols, to develop a culture, to plan ahead, to invent out of necessity, and to make the necessary discoveries needed to change

What accounts for the brain system's ability to function with purpose and direction is totally reliant upon a combination of *neuronal activity* and the *genetic assemblages* that prevailed and became permanently established over time throughout its evolutionary development. Darwin's theory of evolution (Natural Selection) provides us with an explanation of how this came to be.

While it is true that an individual's brain system relies heavily upon neuronal experiences acquired from its surroundings for its maturation, the *development* of the brain system over the course of countless generations can be directly tied to whatever genetic assemblages happened to exist and prevailed during that period of time, in that the genetic ensembles that exist in the human brain system today can be traced back in time as resulting from the process of "natural selection" involving our most distant ancestors. For example, if the brain system of one of our primate ancestors happened to have had a particular genetic assemblage that allowed it to detect the movement of a predator in high grass and in turn to have successfully escaped it, it could be said that that ancestor possessed the necessary psycho-biological *programming* needed to survive such an experience. On the other hand, a primate who lacked such an attribute, generally ended up as a meal for the predator, in that its particular psycho-biological programming was inadequate. And so, over time, those ancestors who lacked the psycho-biological means for survival perished, while those who possessed it survived, and as survivors, they subsequently passed on their "successful" gene assemblages to the next generation, the next, and so on. Thus, by the process of "natural selection," (survival of the fittest) the best of genetic assemblages were being carried on while the inferior ones were eventually eliminated. Meaning, if you're alive and kicking today, you can rest assured that your brain is carrying around the very best of "successful" gene assemblages Nature has been able to put together because they've passed the test of time, change, and "natural selection." Okay?

As for the brain's neuronal activity, that's another matter. It's what ties the brain system' together. It is the establishment and existence of the billions of nerve cells linked in neuronal networks that provides your brain system with the means to be responsive and initiative, both to its own *system* and the environment that surrounds it. It's interesting to note that a newborn child has more neurons available to establish networks in its brain than at any other time in its life, and that unless its brain is stimulated early in infancy with sufficient enriching experiences (Milwaukee Project, next chapter) to establish networks needed to handle it, its excessive neurons are genetically programmed to die off to the point that they satisfy the brain's needs at the time. What's significant about this, of course, is that the greater the number of networks established early in life, the greater is the capacity of the brain system to retain data as memory and to thereby function more expeditiously.

For those of you who don't know, a nerve cell ...a neuron... consists of a cell body containing a *nucleus,* branching receptor fibers called dendrites, and a long transmitting fiber called an *axon.* All functions of the brain system are the result of the activity of many, many, neurons linked together in networks working with still other networks. Communication in the system is carried out by electrical signals sent along one neuron's axon to the receptive dendrites of another. Where they make contact is called a *synapse,* a tiny cleft or fissure, where electrical signals are converted into a chemical code. As a result of the code, a chemical substance is released allowing the message to "slide" across the synaptic fissure and continue its journey to a specialized receptor on another neuron. Once received it is acted upon, be it a command to raise the body blood pressure, move an arm or leg, think a thought, or whatever.

So much for the brain's development. Now, let's turn to how the brain system functions in terms of why you and I think and behave as we do.

YOUR SYSTEM

In that this chapter is the *key stone* of what this book is about, I feel it would behoove you to know exactly what it is we are about to be dealing with, primarily because there seems to be some confusion as to *what your mind is.* As you know, reference to "mind" has been around since before the birth of Christ. We're all familiar with it. We all use the term, "mind." We all claim to be "mindful" of this or that. Some of us even claim to have two "minds" ...a conscious and a subconscious. So what is "mind," anyway? Is it a part of our brain? Is it something we use to control our brain? Or is it something ethereal?

Personally, for many years I considered my mind to be an entity that consciously linked me to my brain wherein I was able to control it; that is, until I looked up the definition of mind in the dictionary, which left me somewhat confused; the confusion being, that all the dictionaries I've consulted defined the mind in terms of what it "does," not what it "is." The same was true of defining "mental," in that it including an added inference that anything mental has to do "with" the mind. For example, "the mind" is defined: as *memory,* as that which *thinks,* that which *perceives and understands,* that which is a *conscious experience,* that which is *unconscious,* that which *can be directed,* that *which is intelligent,* etc. On the other hand anything to do with "mental" is defined: as *of or for the mind or intellect; done by, or carried on in, the mind.* Well, in my opinion, if something can be carried on "in" the mind, then the mind would certainly have to be an entity, wouldn't it? But it isn't, at least according to the dictionary it isn't.

So let's clear up the confusion. In light of the lack of any authority inferring that the mind is an entity, and the fact that mind is defined in terms as stated above, it would seem logical to me to assume then, that properly defined, the mind is: "something the brain does." And in order to avoid any further confusion, if and whenever any idioms are used by me, such as "keeping in mind," "being mindful of," "impressing your mind," etc., they should be regarded as but expressions pertaining to *what the brain does*. Okay?

YOUR BRAIN SYSTEM

The first thing to understand about your brain is *what it is*. More than just three pounds of neurons and glial matter; your brain is essentially a *system* made-up of complexes consisting of three interdependent brains that exists within a closed system comprised of six information-gathering receptors, and a supportive body that houses and maintains the system. The three-brain complex consists of the evolutionary brain stem ...the Medulla Obligonta ...associated with our reptilian ancestry, the Cerebellum ...associated with our mammalian ancestry, and the Cerebrum ...the highest order of brain development known today. The six receptor complex is comprised of your sensors of sight, sound. taste, touch, smell and intuition. And the structure that accommodates, supports and houses the complete system of complexes consists of all the physiological and autonomical parts that make-up the human body. As an enclosed entity, the brain system is self-contained and self-sufficient to the point that it is equipped and structured to handle anything that's needed in order for it to respond intelligently to both itself and the environment surrounding it in a logical and purposeful fashion.

Now, if I've painted the picture properly for you, you should consider both *you* and your brain system as follows: Every time you stand in front of the mirror and admire that beautiful Herculean and/or Venus body of your's(?), what you're actually seeing is nothing more than a supportive structure designed by Nature to accommodate and house your brain system and its supportive complexes ...the inference being that you and your brain system are one-in-the-same; that the essence of *you* lies within.

LEARNING MACHINE

According to some scientists, our brain is the most complex machine in the known universe. And so it is. In simple terms, however, it can be described as a self-contained, goal-seeking "learning machine." It is self-contained in the sense that it arrives into its new world environment with all the innate biological systems and programming it needs in order to survive. Its survival depends heavily upon what it "learns" from its new surroundings through the aid of its sensors, in that they unrelentlessly gather data or information from their surroundings, the experiences of which are recorded and filed away in the brain's memory system, whereupon the data is used as a source of reference in the assessment of each ensuing experience that follows. In other words, in order for your brain to "learn" how to survive and deal successfully with both itself and its new environment, it relies on three parts of its system to do what it does: its *sensory complex* to provides it with on-going data pertaining to both its system and its surroundings; a retrievable *memory complex* that records and stores all data gathered by its sensors; and a *data processing complex* (part of the brain complex) from which all decisions are made for the system to be carried out accordingly.

As mentioned earlier, when we speak of our mind we're not talking about some entity in our brain, but rather about a process of what our brain does that entails the interplay of billions of nerve cells and their respective processes; events within our brain system that when suitably transformed and interpreted within certain areas of the brain produce a "thoughtful awareness" of what our brain is doing. Obviously we are not "thoughtfully" aware of every single event taking place in our brain, for if we were, we would undoubtedly spend our waking hours undergoing a continuous epileptic fit. But we don't, and fortunately, to a great degree, we can be selective about our thoughts. For example, from your own experiences you know it's not normal to be *thoughtfully* aware of, say the big toe on the left foot or the little finger on the right hand and what it is doing while walking about. Yet, as you also know, you can opt to direct your thoughts to just about any part of your body and consciously sense its status as well as direct it to do something in particular. Why the option? It would seem that, as a result of time, change and selection (evolution), Nature found that running and maintaining a "system," such as yours and mine, is best attended to by genetically programmed older brains designed to work at a level below consciousness (subconscious), thus freeing up the conscious aspect of the enlarged newer brain to deal with the more pressing matters of *intuition and critical analysis;* a sort of hierarchical organization if you will, like a ship, captain and crew analogy wherein each level takes orders from the level above it, and each unit in each level goes about its duties without concern for what the other units are doing. In other words, it seems Nature found it more expedient to leave the duties of running and maintaining the "system" to an analogous crew at a subconscious level and let the analogous captain make the decisions we share with our brain at a consciouos level, all of which brings us to how your brain system can be thought to carry out its functions.

For the sake of simplicity, it might be helpful to think of your brain complex as operating at both levels of conscious and subconscious. For example, under the general heading of your Subconscious, it would include your *sensory* complex, your *memory* complex, and your *operative* complex that runs and maintains the system. And operating under the general heading of your Conscious would be that part of your processing complex you share a conscious relationship with as it pertains to all critical decision-making for *the* system. We'll begin with the Subconscious aspect of your brain system relationship.

THE SUBCONSCIOUS

The Subconscious is appropriately called what it is because it carries-out its functions at a level below conscious awareness. Its more important functions entail the maintenance and operation of the brain's complexes of *operative, memory and sensory* as follows:

To control and regulate all the "autonomic" and involuntary functions of the body system associated with the "reptilian" part of the brain, such as heartbeat, blood pressure, respiration, swallowing, sexual drive, glandular secretions, etc. as-well-as those associated with the "mammalian" brain, such as moods, emotions, love, affection, body coordination, etc. And even when your conscious state of awareness is altered, whether due to sleep, hypnosis or a concussion, to continue to control and regulate the brain's system functions as circumstances dictate.

To faithfully record and store in its *memory* complex all the data it receives from both within and outside your brain system as transmitted to it by its *sensory* complex. And, as a part of its memory storage capability, to formulate automatic or pre-programmed courses of action or thought into prescribed *patterns of habit,* such as learning and remembering the multipication tables, playing the piano, grooving a golf swing, likes and dislikes, etc.

Within the memory complex of your Subconscious lies a record of all the data or information pertaining to everything your sensors have experienced since your inception. From the extent of this accumulation of acquired knowledge, your Subconscious provides your processing complex with the kind of information it needs in order to carry-out its processing and decision-making, including what its purpose and direction should be in terms of concepts describing what your best interests are in terms of your likes, dislikes, your fears, etc. Your Subconscious is also responsible for accessing the kind of information needed in order for it to maintain your sanity in the form of dreams as well as providing creative solutions to your problems.

Probably the most significant aspect about your Subconscious memory complex is its total inability to discriminate between, say, an imagined experience and one that is real, in that whatever its sensors are experiencing is accepted as *fact* and in turn faithfully recorded at *face value* in memory regardless of how distorted it may be ...a characteristic of the utmost importance of which will become obvious to you in a later chapter.

THE CONSCIOUS

As for the Conscious aspect of your brain system, we are not referring to a part of your brain, but rather as a "mindful" awareness of "sitting in" on the processing being carried-out by your processing complex; a center that's essentially *in charge* of your entire brain system. It's the conscious awareness of some of the activities on the part of your processing complex that provides us with a sense of being and living in an unfolding world; an awareness that translates into our thoughts and considerations, our doubts and fears, our likes and dislikes, our goals, our best interests, and the nature of what sort of decisions need to be made.

Considering the complexity of your over-all brain function in comparison to that which we regard as conscious awareness, I would say that the conscious aspect of your brain system accounts for very little, in that it has but one essential function to perform for your over-all brain system: that of *critical analysis,* and to deal intelligently with any and all data or information pertaining to your instincts, such as a possible *threat* to your *survival,* or the possibiity of experiencing *unfavorable recognition or appreciation.* Meaning, that whatsoever experiences are picked up by any one of your sensors, each poses a potential threat to your system's well-being. In order to deal intelligently with any such threat, your Conscious needs information before it can make its decision. And the only available array of such information lies within the memory files of your Subconscious, which maintains a record of essentially everything you have *personally* experienced since birth ...and possibly even before that.

With this in mind, then, your Conscious (your processing complex) can then be thought to carrying-out its function of decision-making by following these four steps:

1. *To identify* all data received by your Subconscious sensors as representing a possible threat to your system.

2 *To compare* its findings of the possible *threatening data* with like or similar experiences of record in your memory.

3 *To evaluate* the identified/compared findings on the basis of established "guidelines" in your memory defining what your best interests are.

4 *To make a decision* for responsive action or inaction based upon the outcome of its evaluation.

A simple working example of how your Conscious carries out these four steps of processing is to imagine yourself sitting in your living room, relaxed and reading a book. The door bell rings. Your sound *sensor* alerts your Conscious to a ringing sound ...interrupting your reading. In response your Conscious directs your Subconscious to quickly run through its memory files to *identify* the possible *threatening* data. Your Subconscious identifies it as the door bell. Your Conscious, in response, asks your Subconscious to *compare* the threatening door bell data with other comparable data of record in its memory files. Your Subconscious comes back in response that it's a signal someone is at the front door, and that recent memory files indicate you are in the living room and your wife is in the hall near the front door hanging up some clothes. All of this information is rapidly *evaluated* by your Conscious, leading to a *decision* that it would be in your *best interests* for it to direct your Subconscious to instruct your vocal chords to say, "Hey, sweetheart, get the front door will you, please?"

Each of us spends all of our waking hours with our Conscious running through these four steps of identification, comparison, evaluation, and decision. The process is exceedingly rapid, and perfectly accurate. And only two things can lead to a decision, or action, which is not in your best interest. One is failing to sense something ...perhaps due to failing eyesight or hearing, or to having blocked-out your awareness due to a case of deep concentration. The other would be that of one of your sensors transmitting inaccurate information to your Subconscious. For example, if the air line information clerk tells you on the phone that flight 1549 is scheduled to leave at 10:15 p.m., and you arrive at the airport at 9:45 only to find that the plane left at 8:15, then your directed action was wrong only because the data made available to your Subconscious was false ...something we older folk refer to as "having a senior moment." Okay?

MEMORY

More than anything else, it is the data of record in your memory that has everything to do with how you conduct yourself at any moment in your life. For instance, did you ever give any thought as to why a baby is so helpless at birth? Assuming its brain and sensors are operative, did you ever wonder why it can't carry on a conversation? why it can't control its bladder and bowels? why it can't feed itself? why it can't walk or run? Hey, I'm serious! Does its helplessness have anything to do with its ethnic background? No! Does it have anything to do with the intelligence of its parents? No! Does it have anything to do with its genetic make up? No! How then do you explain a newborn's helplessness we all take for granted? One reason only. Even though a newborn's brain system is prepared to carrying out its normal function, it is unable to do so because at birth it *lacks* the necessary data or information (knowledge) needed to perform the above. In other words, lacking the necessary information in its memory due to lack of experience, the newborn's Conscious is totally unaware of how to deal with such things.

Understandably, in the early days of the learning process there is little or no reference data of record in the infant's memory system because its sensors have had little time to experience anything in its new environment. But after a month or so, and after some past experiences have been repeated to the point that they gain some prominence in its memory ...such as repeatedly seeing its parents' faces and the sound of their voices night and day.. its Conscious is readily able to distinguish its parents from strangers. The same holds true of other experiences as well, in that the more data of record in the infant's memory pertaining to a particular experience, the more prominent it becomes compared to lessor experienced data. Thus the more influence it will have on its Conscious when dealing with like or similar experiences.

As an infant's environment begins to expand, so does the variety of experiences and record of them in memory expand accordingly. Before long the infant's memory files contain sufficient knowledge to formulate a variety of concepts pertaining to its past experiences to the point that its Conscious is able to carry on such things as conversation, control of its bladder and bowels, to feed itself, to walk and run; not because of its ethnic background, not because of the intelligence of its parents or genetic make up, but as a result of what it has learned *solely from what it has personally experienced from its surroundings.* More specifically, it is the more *prominent* of data in memory that formulate the necessary guidelines needed by your Conscious in order to deal intelligently with both its system and its surroundings.

To better understand how these guidelines have evolved and how they affect your mind's decisions, it's necessary that you first have a mental picture of what your memory complex is all about. Making it as simple as possible, your memory system can be thought to be comparable to a gigantic version of the array of room-key/mail slots readily visible behind the main desk of a hotel, and every time your sensors alert your Subconscious to something, the experience of it is *faithfully* recorded on a slip of paper and placed in one of these slots. And further, just like it is at the post office when mail to the same address is placed in the same slot, so it is with your memory slots; every tangible reception relating to a particular previous experience is placed in the same slot.

Now, with this in mind, consider how the memory complex of an infant might appear at birth. Because of limited experiences impressed upon its memory while in the womb, its memory slots will be pretty much empty in the beginning. Then, within a short time after birth, due to the infant sensing happenings taking place around it, slips of data will begin appearing in a random number of memory slots. And then, as further happenings are experienced during the ensuing days, weeks, and months, the amount of slips in particular slots will increase many-fold while other slots might contain but a few, and still other slots might contain only one, but of a different color.

What's significant about a single colored slip and many slips in the same slot as compared to the other slots containing three or four slips, is that they attract more attention from the Subconscious because they stand-out from the rest. And because of their prominence, they command more attention from the Subconscious than the other less conspicuous. But before we get into the consequences of prominence, let me first explain how certain data acquires its prominence over other data.

PROMINENCE

There are but two ways in which data acquires its prominence in memory. The first is by *repetition*. The other is by *emotional association*. For example, were you, as a child to pick-up a basketball and attempt to shoot it through a hoop, hypothetically the data accounting for the experience would undergo processing, be recorded on a slip of paper, and placed in one of the slots in memory. Were you to repeat the experience, the repeated experience would undergo the same processing, be recorded on another slip of paper, and placed along side the previous experience in the same slot. Were you to continue repeating the same experience, over a period of time it wouldn't be long before there would be many slips of paper in the same slot. Thus, the fact that there are many slips in one slot as opposed to only one in another, the slot containing many slips would stand-out compared to a slot containing only one ...a case of prominence acquired by *repetition*.

By contrast, were you to have a once-only experience of being attacked and severely bitten by a dog, the data accounting for the experience, too, would be recorded on a single sheet of paper and wind-up in a slot in memory. But unlike the basketball experiences, it would warrant a colored slip, say, red, because of the *emotional* factor associated with it. And because of its color, it would command at least as much attention as that of a slot containing many slips of paper. The degree of prominence of any data stored in your memory, then, is effected either by *repetition* and/or *emotion*. Okay? Now back to the consequences of what prominent data in your memory produces.

PURPOSE AND DIRECTION

Learning what its purpose and direction is has been an evolving thing for your brain system since birth. It began when the first bits of *prominent* data started appearing in your memory. Like the attention-getting road signs along the highway suggesting you slow down to a certain speed on a curve, the more prominent data worked in the same way in catching the attention of your Subconscious, whereupon it was passed on to your Conscious and used as criteria or as a *guideline* in helping it to deal intelligently with each new impending experience brought to its attention. Such was how, as an infant, your brain was able to deal with your immediate surrounding with some sense of purpose and direction.

As time passed and the scope of your surroundings began to expand at a rapid pace, so did the formulation of a variety of guidelines take shape in your memory as a consequence, expressing such things as your likes, your dislikes, your hopes and fears, your opinions, your goals, your attitudes about yourself and your surroundings.

Before long, the demands placed on your Conscious by the cumulative number of guidelines became so varied, that like trying to accommodate the wishes of each individual in a crowd, your Subconscious collectively incorporated them under one umbrella, so to speak, that expressed a general over-all concept that exemplified what your Conscious was to take into account in determining what was best for your system in terms of purpose and direction. Such a concept can be regarded as your Self-Concept; a generalized conception that defines the status of your brain system to itself, including setting the limits on just how responsive and creative you can become.

SELF CONCEPT

What's so important about your Self-Concept ...as it is with the individual guidelines that account for it... is that its influence is totally responsible for the *nature* of your thoughts and behavior. Every decision your Conscious makes for you, every action your Conscious initiates, is carried-out according to your Self-Concept. Other than the memory of what you've experienced in the past, the data defining your Self-Concept has much to do with controlling your life! And it does so through the substance of your thoughts. It accounts for the mental picture of how you view yourself and your capabilities at any moment in your life.

A good analogy of how your Self-Concept affects every facet of your life can be related to the thermostat that controls the furnace in your home. As you know, a thermostat is linked directly to the furnace, and depending upon the temperature setting *purposely* selected, the furnace will turn itself on and off, striving to maintain the setting. When the room temperature reaches the specific setting, the furnace shuts down. And when the room starts to cool down, the furnace turns back on again. In either case, turning on or off, the furnace does its job by maintaining the temperature *selected by you*. And so it is with your Conscious as it attempts *to make decisions in its (your) best interest* by striving to direct your thoughts and actions in accordance with the "setting" as defined by your Self-Concept.

Perhaps you can recall certain periods in your life when it seemed like everything was coming-up roses, and then, for no apparent reason, the bubble burst and you found yourself wondering why everything had suddenly turned sour. Such an effect was not without cause. What you had experienced during these periods was analogous to the thermostat controlling the furnace: the result of your Conscious initiating thoughts to literally "shut you down," so to speak; striving to keep you within the limits defined by your Self-Concept "setting."

Equally so, perhaps you can recall those periods when nothing seemed to be going right for you and you were ready to "throw in the towel." In such a situation you had literally fallen below your Self-Concept setting, and so, in response, your Conscious "went to the whip," so to speak, and tried to boost you up by causing you to think and behave in a manner above and beyond your *normal* frame of mind. As a result of the momentum brought about by your "altered" state of mind, you were carried above and beyond the limits of your Self-Concept "setting," finding yourself "on top of the world." Unfortunately, you didn't remain there long because your Conscious all too soon perceived that you had surpassed your "setting" and thereby literally shut down your whole system, waiting for you to drop back to your "normal" setting.

The momentum of coming down was no different than that of going up; you surpassed the setting. When you had passed it, like all good goal-oriented brain systems, it fired you up again in order to get your thoughts back in line with the picture "you hold of yourself" ...in accordance with your Self Concept. And so it has been for each of us, day by day, month by month, year by year, happy days and discouraging days; the direct result of our brain system directing our thoughts and behavior, striving to keep us within the limits "set" by our Self-Concept. Okay?

Now, since your understanding of what your Conscious does for you is "the" key to enlightenment of subject matter to follow, let's quickly review the more important aspects of what we've covered so far.

Summation

As mentioned earlier, when we speak of "mind", we're not referring to an entity; we're speaking of a "process" by which *the brain system does what it does.* When you and I were born ...no matter who are parents were or where it occurred on planet Earth ...we arrived into this world possessing a wondrous brain system that after some 4-billion years of experimenting in terms of time, change, and selection represents the best that Nature has to offer; a brain system that Nature has psycho-biochemically programmed with its most successful genetic ensembles that provided it with the means to deal successfully with its surroundings in a logical and purposeful fashion.

To successfully carry out its mission of survival, pro-creation, and to be the best it can become after birth requires that the brain system be *informed* of what's taking place in its new surroundings. For this it is *totally dependent* and relies *solely* upon its sensors of sight, sound, taste, touch, smell, and intuition.

To successfully deal with the data the brain system receives from its sensors requires that the data be retained in the form of *memory* (acquired knowledge) whereupon it can be used by its *processing complex* as a source of *reference* in dealing with each new bit of ensuing data it receives ...a case of applying what is learned (in terms of success or failure) from one experience and applying it to another, and another to another, and so on.

Shortly after birth, and with a continuous flow of new data being assimilated in memory, certain data begins to take on varying degrees of *prominence* over other data in memory as a result of the brain's sensors *repeatedly experiencing* the same happening or experiencing a one-time happening accompanied by a high degree of *emotion,* both of which impart data with "stand-out" status among the other data in memory. Due to their stand-out prominence, these data naturally command more attention from the Conscious (processing complex), and in so doing add still further to their degree of prominence. As a result of their prominence, these particular data serve to provide the processing complex with guidance in the form of concepts which they and other conceptual data that follows in turn serve to provide it with the *purpose and direction* it needs in order to respond to both the body housing the system and the environment surrounding it in a logical and purposeful fashion. But, as we all know, the purpose and direction portrayed by some peoples' brain complex is often questionable ...as in the case of those who are involved in such things as crime, violence and drug abuse.

So why the discrepancy? Why do some peoples' brain direct them to become high achievers, while others' brains direct them to be mediocre or to pursue a life of crime and violence? The simple answer is: It's not the brain complex, itself, that defines what an individual will do or become, it is, rather, the *nature* of the data representing *what has been experienced and made a part of memory* that provides the *instructive data* to the processing complex that *defines* what the brain system is *compelled* to achieve.

By Nature's design, all brain systems are formed and function as a *mechanism;* a system whose parts work together like a machine. The brain system does what it does with purpose and direction, whether conscious or unconscious, using cause-and-effect logic based *solely* upon data it receives *solely* from what its sensors gathered *solely* from its own surroundings and becomes retained *solely* in its own memory.

The bottom-line difference between every member of the human race ...in terms of what they think and how they behave... is directly related to the *nature* of the data of record in their respective memory systems. Those who become involved in a life of crime and violence, those who live a life of mediocracy, and those who become high achievers, do so as a result of what they've experienced in the past. It can be no other way! Our brain system is a mechanism that initiates and responds *solely in accordance with the data made available to it* ...all of which adds up to a very simple fact when it comes to understanding and assessing both ourselves and others, a fact which happens to be the central theme of this book: We are what we are at any time in our life because of what we've experienced in the past. Aside from that, all members of humanity are essentially the same.

Okay, you should now have a partial "key" as to *who* you are and *why* you are what you are today? As I said, it's only a partial key, and hopefully you will apply it diligently to what's to follow; I say diligently because I'm sure your brain system, better known as your "system," will tend to dispute some of what's to follow ...as is probably the case with what we've just covered due to the influence of the *nature* of *your* past experiences   In any event, stick around for the finish. It'll change your life completely ...and for the better. I guarantee it!

MYTH OR NURTURE

We are a product of everything we have experienced

Typically, boy Dick and girl Jane get married. They have children; two boys, 3 years apart. In the course of growing up one boy goes to college and becomes a computer expert. The other boy quits in his last year of high school and eventually winds-up working at a fast-food restaurant. Both claim to be happy in what they're doing. The question often asked is, how can two members of the same family, brought up in essentially the same surroundings, turn out so different? I'm sure the same question has crossed the minds of countless families all over the world: What causes one child to do one thing and another to do something else?

Can it be explained? Some have certainly tried. One school of thought insists it's a matter of heredity, while another claims it's a case of environment. This, of course, explains nothing; it only offers a choice, and depending upon which school of thought you choose to believe can greatly influence your prospects of what the future holds for you. For example, should you choose to believe that you are what you are because of what you have inherited from your parents, you're in effect saying your life is preordained and there's little or nothing you can do about changing it; the die is cast, so to speak; you're limited according to the nature of your genes. On the other hand, should you choose to believe that what you do in life is directly influenced by what you experience from your environment, you're not so limited because there is always the possibility that you can make constructive changes in your life merely by being more selective about what you experience from your surroundings. In light of these opposing view points, suppose we consider the facts:

Probably the greatest misconception people generally have about the human experience is the illusion that some people are born into this world inherently smarter, better and more capable than others. This is especially true when it comes to the white majority comparing itself with other groups. For instance, if you happen to be in the majority, it seems that all you have to do is look around and let the facts speak for themselves, i.e., Who's doing the menial jobs? Who's committing most of the crimes? Who's collecting most of the welfare checks and food stamps? Who represents the highest unemployment rate? Who are the least educated? Etcetera. Etcetera.

It certainly can't be denied there is a propensity of minority groups involved in the lower socio-economic status of our country. But to suppose that it is directly related to one's bio-genetic background is ludicrous and smacks of ignorance, because if it were true ...that genetic inheritance is responsible for one's socio-economic status... few, if any, of the white majority would make it to first base, because, genetically speaking, there's hardly a person of the white majority who could claim the degree of bio-genetic purity in strain and descendentcy as that enjoyed by any of the minority groups. Compared to the pedigree of the minority, the white majority are mongrels. And just for the record, Homo erectus ...the early ancestor of all races known today... evolved in Africa. And Homo erectus was thought to be black.

SOCIAL-GENES?

Granted, our genetic background is important. But are bio-genes, alone, accountable for one's social and economic status? Or could it be there's another kind of so-called genetic influence ...social in nature... that is passed on from one generation to another just as bio-genes are passed on in determining one's biological self? It's certainly a possibility, especially if these so-called "social-genes" include all the factors that have been misconstrued as being biologically oriented; namely those credited for one's intelligence, degree of achievement, technical know-how, habits, customs, mannerisms, attitudes, beliefs, etc. Suppose we consider the possibilities:

Let's assume two adults ...you and someone of the opposite sex... were set down in some remote part of the world where no man had ever been. Let's also assume that all traces of memorable experiences have been blotted out of your Subconscious memory; that you and your mate are, in essence, at the total mercy of your surroundings ...as was the case of primitive man. Would you and your mate be able to communicate, think, act or cope with your surroundings better than did the most primitive of mankind? It's highly unlikely ...even with the twenty-first century genes you might be carrying... because they hardly differ from those of earlier man.   And deprived of all the possible "social-genes" that could have been acquired and accumulated over many thousands of years, you and your ensuing descendants would have to travel the same long road of social evolution just as the earliest of primitive man did. You would have to begin all over again learning the simplest facts by trial and error. The bottom line being: it would take many generations of learning before you would know how to fashion the simplest of tools, develop a language, plant seeds, construct a dwelling, etc., all of which means: that if any group living today which happens to differ from any group of previous generation in mental development, behavior, or other socio-economic conditions, or happens to be in possession of any superior invention, appliances or objects, it should not be construed as a case of possessing superior bio-genes, but rather because of what had been *learned* and passed on from one generation to the next, ...in the form of "social-genes" inherited "socially" from the past. And while in saying this it should not be thought to infer that the total accumulation of all *learned* "social-genes" have been passed on from one generation to the next, either. Undoubtedly, in many instances, some of the best of the "social-genes" of successive legacies have been lost, destroyed, or foolishly tossed away due to all the wars, barbaric invasions, and blotting-out of entire civilizations; of the whims and judgments of ruling despots that often dictated the course of culture much as it is being dictated in our societies today, thereby suggesting good reason to believe that numerous "social-genes" of inestimable value were not passed on while some of the worst were.

Now, should any one still contemptuously feel that bio-genes are primarily responsible for one's socio-economic status; that *learning-experience* has little to do with it, they will no doubt embrace still another general misconception: that parents of high IQ (intelligence quotient) have off-springs with high IQ; that parents of low IQ have off-springs with low IQ. Let's take a look at some surprising evidence.

ENRICHING THE ENVIRONMENT

According to a 1964 study by the "Milwaukee Project," more than six-million persons in the United States at that time were considered to be mentally retarded, and although the great majority of them had no identifiable pathology of the nervous system, all had exceptionally low IQs, and all were functionally, if not physiologically, retarded. It was also revealed that mentally retarded persons were generally found in particularly large numbers among the population of economically distressed urban and rural areas made-up primarily of minority groups.

Realizing, that by far, the great majority of low socio-economic groups living in slum areas are not retarded, and that the majority of children reared by economically disadvantaged families develop and learn in relatively normal fashion, these facts suggested that the heavy concentration of persons considered to be mentally retarded in the slum areas were related to certain specific factors rather than the general environment, the Milwaukee Project set out to find them.

Their survey revealed that *maternal-intelligence* was the most reliable single indicator of the level and character of intellectual development of the child.   And although mothers with an IQ below 80 made-up less than half the total group of mothers in the study, they accounted for about four-fifths of the children with IQs below 80. The survey data further showed that the lower the mother's IQ the greater the possibility of their children scoring low on intelligence tests, primarily because she *creates a social environment* for her off-spring that is distinctly different from that created by her neighbor of normal IQ level living in the same low socio-economic area.

Armed with these findings, the challenge for the "Project" was to see whether intellectual deficiency might be prevented through the introduction of an array of positive factors in the child's *early* life while at the same time avoiding what could be considered negative or adverse influences.

The experiment began with some 40 mothers with IQs of less than 70 along with their newborn children.   The newborn babies were divided into two groups, with two-thirds of them being placed in the experimental program, and the remaining one-third in a control group. As for the mothers, they made-up one group.

Shortly after a mother returned from the hospital, teachers began visiting her several hours each day, focusing most of their attention upon the infant. Some weeks later both mother and baby joined programs at an Infant Education Center. The infant, usually three to four-months old, was exposed to a wide variety of *mental stimulation* for several hours each day on a one-to-one basis with trained adults. Meanwhile, the mother was encouraged to take part in a Center program designed to teach her improved home-making and baby-care techniques, and in some cases, provided with basic occupational training.

At 24 months, the two-year-olds were placed in a class consisting of five youngsters. At 36 months the size of the class was increased to eight; and at 4 years it was increased to eleven with three teachers assigned to the group.

The findings at 42 months were this: Generally, it was found that the children exposed since infancy to the daily routine of *mental stimulation* showed a remarkable development in contrast with the children in the control group. The children in the active stimulation program measured an average of 33 IQ points *higher* than the children in the control group, with some of them registering IQs as high as 135! Equally remarkable, the children learned at a rate *in excess of the national norm* for their age peers.

It should be of interest to note that this report was issued in 1971. In a 1980 follow-up it was reported that the children involved in the experimental group were still maintaining their 20-to-30 point IQ *advantage* over the control group in spite of the fact they had all entered the public educational system.

The results of the "Project" by no means settle the controversial environment versus heredity, but it does bring to light some points that are important to each of us, especially those who have a low opinion of themselves as to their intelligence, potential and capability to "make it" to the upper rungs of the socio-economic ladder. The fact that you can take a youngster who, if left to develop in surroundings created by a low IQ mother would no doubt mirror her intelligence but is. instead, exposed to mental stimulation *at the outset* and will respond with a mental-dexterity *exceeding* the norm of the country, it would seem to indicate that intelligence is not so much a matter of inheritance as it is to one's social environment, or at least a combination thereof. If this is true, as it certainly appears to be, then whatever degree of low socio-economic status one finds him/herself in today should not necessarily be considered indicative of one's potential and capability, but rather a case of unfortunate environmental circumstances; circumstances that can certainly be changed, but not by the *victims* who are exposed to it, unless, of course, they are educated to the fact that they *can* change it! ...which by now you should know is the sole purpose of this book.

WE'RE ALIKE, YET DIFFERENT

In his book, "Intelligence Can Be Taught", (P. Dutton and CO.), Dr. Arthur Whimbey, associate professor of psychology at Dillard University, contends that intelligence is an important but trainable skill rather than an innate or inherited capacity to learn.

Whimbey's theory was dramatically opposed to that of Arthur Jensen, psychologist at the University of California, who caused a furor in 1969 with his theory that race determines intellectual capacity, and that blacks are inherently (bio-genetically) inferior to whites. Jensen further postulated that compensatory educational programs are bound to fail because children who have inherent low IQs can never master the standard academic curriculum.

Whimbey argues that all normal brain systems are "bio-chemically the same." And that excepting the small percentage of the population who are retarded or brain damaged, "everyone is born equal in terms of basic learning capacity."

We have identical computers," he says, "but some are programmed differently from others." In other words, there is no detectable neurological differences between those who score high on intelligence test and those who do not.

"When IQ begins to emerge," according to Whimbey, "it
is primarily a reflection of the child's environment."
Parents in upper and middle class households tend to value
intellectual thinking as an activity necessary for success in
a literate-technical society. Consequently, they spend time
with their children encouraging them to think and reason
on an intellectual basis. Lower class parents, on the other
hand, seldom have time to converse with their youngsters.
In many cases both parents are working. In others, mothers
are too busy tending the needs of large families to give
individual attention to one child. In still others, the family
consists of a single parent, and more than often who is on
welfare. The end result is that children from different
socio-economic levels, generally develop different degrees
of "information processing skills," which is
"intelligence," according to Whimbey.

When given IQ test, the child who has acquired "some"
intelligence will score higher than the "unintelligent"
child. IQ tests to Whimbey are likened to driving tests.
"Driving, like intelligence, is a learned skill. An IQ test
does not measure innate mental capacity anymore than a
driving test measures innate physical capacity. They both
measure skill very well and are most useful for deciding
who needs more training."

On the basis of Whimbey's contention: that brains are
neurological *identical* and intelligence is purely *a learned
skill,* he assesses a genius as "the result of a combination of
an enormous amount of academic intelligence and an
obsessive interest in a topic. The difference between an
average lawyer and a Clarence Darrow is study and
dedication. "As for the prodigies, he says, "the neurological
system is usually mature at age 16. But just as children
show different physical growth rates, they quite logically
have different neurological growth rates, too. Prodigies are
the product of early neurological growth plus and enormous
intellectual orientation on the part of the family. Studies

show that parents (of prodigies) are bending over backwards
to encourage intellectual growth."

INTELLIGENCE IS ACQUIRED

It seems that Dr. Whimbey is not alone in his theories.
Aaron Stern, a university lecturer who says his system of
total-immersion education prepared his daughter to enter
college at age 12 and become a university mathematics
instructor at age 15, asked the State Department and the
Philippine government to allow him to educate some of the
children of the "Stone Age" Tasaday Tribe, discovered in
the Philippines by the outside world in 1971, in the hope of
documenting that intellectual growth is not dependent on
ethnic or racial origin, and to refute once and for all the
theories of Arthur Jensen and William Shockly (Nobel
Prize-Winning physicist who expounded Jensen's theory).

Stern's plan was to test his educational theories on
children from the remote Tasaday tribe because he believed
their Stone Age culture would be internationally recognized
as a "raw base ...the lowest point on the genetic totem pole,"
more so than, say, the child adopted by French anthropologist
Claude Levi Strauss, who was procured from a primitive
Brazilian Indian tribe, raised and educated in Europe, and
who subsequently graduated Cum Laude from the Sorbonne
University in Paris.

Stern has tested his methods on his own children, and
believes his daughter, Edith, is proof of his success.

Edith, a cyberneticist, was subjected to Stern's "social-
gene" theory from birth. As an infant she heard classical
music 24 hours a day, engendering "nobility," according to
Stern. At age 2 she began to read, and by age 5 she had
absorbed 24 volumes of Encyclopedia Britannica.

Stern assumes that intellectual grow begins at birth and
ends at death. It involves the utilization of all resources.
When Edith wanted to go to the park, she and her father often

passed different sites under construction from which she learned the elements of physics. If they encountered a labor strike, from it she became acquainted with civics. Strolling on the beach she learned the meaning of infinity. From the stars she learned astronomy. From her family she learned love and serenity.

School authorities, as well as other *ignorant* do-gooders (my opinion), have vehemently opposed Stern's methods of education warning it would have ill affects upon any child. Edith does not agree. She says she endorses her father's methods, and believes any one could advance as rapidly as she if they were given similar opportunity. She even expressed surprise that beyond "the usual inertia and resistance to change, some people actually seem frightened of learning."

Unfortunately, to my knowledge Stern has yet to be successful in his request to carry-out his experiment with the Tasadays. The Philippine government's excuse for turning down his request is that the education would have adverse affect upon the tribe, and that they should be left alone in their natural habitat where the world could "learn" much from studying them. Perhaps this is true. But I can't help but think of the overwhelming good that would come out of it were he allowed to prove his point; especially to those who persist in thinking that blood-line genetic inheritance is everything.

I must agree with Edith. Some people, especially those blocking Stern's efforts, actually seem " ... frightened of learning." Were Stern successful in showing the world that a child can be removed from a Stone Age environment of genetically pure lineage and turned into something short of a genius through applied learning, think of the positive affect it would have on people world-wide. People would no longer have an excuse for thinking they were racially or genetically inferior. They would be faced with the reality that although no two people are bio-genetically exactly alike,

they are, in a sense, the same, in that through the acquisition
of knowledge, each and everyone of us can do and become
anything we desire and subsequently rise to the upper level
of any socio-economic ladder.

WE LEARN IN DIFFERENT WAYS

In another vain, as it applies to Dr. Whimbey's
"acquired skill of intelligence," Dr. Taglianneti, of Los
Angeles County Unified Schools, had this to say about
learning: He believed, by and large, the degree by which
intelligence is acquired rests upon the way in which
knowledge is presented to our youngsters; in that some learn
best *verbally* (auditorily) while others learn best *visually*.

According to the Dr., 55-60% of the children starting out
in life learn primarily by visual means ...by reading the
printed words; that 25-30% learn verbally ...by listening;
and that 10-15% are multi-faceted ...learning equally well,
either visually or verbally.

He pointed out that 90% of the words in our language are
configurational ...are formed according to syntax, and that
10% are phonetic, yet we have 42 rules on how to pronounce
phonetic words. A visual-learner, therefore, can learn 100%
of our words, while the verbal-learner, even with a high IQ,
can only learn 10% auditorily ...only if he/she does
exceptionally well!

In Dr. Taglianneti's opinion, the standard method of
teaching is wrong. What it amounts to, is that we
inadvertently suppress and penalize the verbal-learner,
thereby making it difficult for them to read, which in turn
leads to further difficulties in all other fields of
achievement. "In failing to recognize the verbal-learner,"
he said, "we have created the problem. We call them
failures because they cannot communicate without talking.
And what do we do when they talk in class? We tell them to
shut up and *read* to themselves."

According to Dr. Taglianneti, we are "punishing our kids because they have difficulty learning due to the way we (the educators) are *taught* to teach. Articulation out in the real world is basically verbal. Eighty percent of an executive's time is spent auditorily, yet the verbal student, who is not able to learn as well (under our present system) becomes the anti-social child in most instances." The Dr. went on to say, "Crime and violence is connected with the inability to read, and therefore, to learn."

The Dr. did some research on this matter at a number of the prisons in the state. If I remember correctly, he discovered that a sizable majority of the prisoners were audio-learners. Is there a message here? Amen, Dr. Taglianneti!

Summation

If the findings of Dr. Taglianneti, the Milwaukee Project, Dr. Whimbey and Aaron Stern are valid, it would seem then, that a person's character, degree of intelligence and level of achievement is not so much determined by the inheritance factor as it is by *acquisition.* And provided this is correct, it indicates that the potential for outstanding character, high intelligence and remarkable achievement, like a seed, is as much an innate part of every one's inheritance as is the spark of life, itself. As to whether or not all individuals bring this seed to fruition, however, is another matter, because such is directly related to the extent to which their environment *influences them to do so.*

Hopefully by now you are at least aware that there is considerable doubt that heredity, alone, defines the limits of what you can expect to achieve in your life. If you're not, I strongly suggest you consider the case of Susan, age 13, who a social worker discovered confined to her room and kept in diapers all her life, existing on a diet of Pablum and milk, and having the mentality of a 1-1/2 year-old. You might ask yourself this: Was it her bio-genetic inheritance that accounted for her status, or was it the influence of the particular environment forced upon her by her parents? And the children of low IQ mothers who scored high IQs, was their's a case of tapping a potential innate to each and everyone of us through early conditioning, or, by some miracle, were these children born with different genes from their parents? Is it because certain primitive Indian tribes in Brazil pass on better genes than those passed on in the ghettos of America, that a child taken at random from the jungle and exposed to an enriching environment eventually graduated Cum Laude from a world-renowned university? And is it solely because of "good" genes that parents who believe in total-immersion education commencing at birth produced a teacher of college-level mathematics at age 15?

Frankly I think the heredity/environment controversy can be settled with one simple statement: People do, in fact, inherit their intellectual capacity, but not in the sense as advocated by the likes of Jensen and Shockly. It is rather a case of each of us being born with essentially the same degree of potential and capability, but what we do in utilizing it depends entirely upon *the nature of the environment we are involved with during our early years of development.* And as for why two members of the same family turn out so different in spite of the fact both are brought up in essentially the same environment, I think it can be answered in much the same way: Innately, both boys can possess the same degree of "inherent-genetic" potential and capability, but as Dr. Whimbey points out, "just as children show different physical growth rates, they quite logically have different neurological growth rates, also." Subjected to essentially the same environment, each boy is going to react differently to it because of their neurological differences; in that what might turn one child on ...excelling in the class room, for instance... might not "turn-on" the other who happens to excel on the sporting field. And depending upon the amount of parent and peer pressure to conform ...without taking into account their neurological differences... it could cause the gap to widen even further.

The fact that we grow, both physically and neurologically, at individual rates; the fact that no two people can experience the exact same happening in exactly the same way, i.e., seeing a glass of water as being half-empty or half-full; and the fact that there is a recognized difference in how people learn, i.e., visually versus auditorily, should give us sufficient insight as to why no two people think and behave exactly the same. Each of us comes into this world in possession of the necessary potential and capability to become high achievers. The degree to which we utilize it, however, is directly related to *the arsenal of knowledge we acquired as a result of what we personally experience from our surroundings.*

THOUGHTS ARE THINGS

Unless we control our thoughts, our thoughts will control us.

It is written in the Buddhist text: "All that we are is the result of what we have thought." I realize, of course, there are those of you who don't agree, choosing, perhaps, to believe that the cause lies elsewhere, especially in light of the fact, that for most of us, thought has been regarded as a rather ethereal thing; that it lacks substance. Well, so it might have seemed yesterday. But that's history. With the advancement of certain technologies today, we have conclusive evidence that thoughts, sensations, and emotions *physically* exist, since they produce electro-bio-chemical changes in the state of the brain, as can be attested to by viewing PET scans and the measured differences in glucose, oxygen, and other nutrients that vary according to a change in one's mental state. What's significant about this is that it goes a long way in explaining much of the so-called dubious phenomena associated with thought; something we'll be touching upon in just a moment.

I think the key to understanding what thought can accomplish lies with an enlightenment of *what* makes us tick. Clinically speaking, as mentioned earlier, you and I are essentially an electro-biochemical mechanism ...as is all of life as we know it to be. I'll give you an example of what this entails. Let's say it crossed your mind to touch the stove top to see if it had cooled down, and it turned out to be searing hot. In doing so, one or more of your sensory "touch" *cells* would sense a change in temperature and chemically encode the message, whereupon it would be converted to an electrical impulse to the point it reached the brain, where it would in turn be converted back to chemical code and translated. Once translated the brain's reaction would be chemically encoded, converted to an electrical impulse to the point it reached the appropriate muscles, whereupon the signal would be converted back to a chemical code instructing the muscles to remove your hand from the stove. Further, in that some skin *cells* had been damage or destroyed, messages from the carnage, too, would be received by the brain, followed by instructions to other parts of the body and brain to repair the damage. The point? Simply this: Since the brain system functions of reaching out and touching a hot stove top are carried-out on the same electro-biochemical basis as the thoughts responsible for initiating the event in the first place, then it's logical to assume that *any* purposeful thought can bring about *purposeful* electro-biochemical changes in both the brain and the system that houses it. And so it can.

THE POWER OF SUGGESTION

Hypnotism is a subject most people tend to shy away from. Do you know why? Sure you do. At some stage in life those people "caught" a concept ...from their family, school, the media; their surroundings... that hypnotism was evil, the work of the devil, the occult, etc., as was the case for me when I was younger. Such an attitude is not without cause, however, because hypnotism has been exploited in every possible way since the beginning of the twentieth century ...mostly bad! People fear it mainly because of their ignorance of what it is, or because what they were told was distorted. Ironically, however, each and every one of us is involved with hypnotism up to our ear lobes every moment of our wakeful life and don't know it!

Properly defined, hypnotism is nothing more than the *control of thought and action through suggestion.* In this case, suggestion would include anything that can be perceived through the aid of one's sensors: a mother lulling her child to sleep with soft spoken words or song; the incessant half-truths and rhetoric put out by the government, politicians, the press, radio, TV, publications, religious institutions, what you're reading this very moment. All is suggestion! And all suggestion is hypnotism! All is carried-out for a specific reason: to influence the thoughts and actions of the spectator-listeners, viewers, and readers accordingly. If you have any doubts about this truth, just look around. Is there anywhere you can't go without being subjected to the power of suggestion? Even if you escape the deluge of suggestion in the big city by seeking refuge in some remote area in the wilderness, such as a running stream, the song of birds, the wild animals frolicking in the meadow; all will work a spell of suggestion upon you. There's no way you can escape suggestion. And no matter who you are or where you go, your thoughts, actions and behavior will be influenced in some way, accordingly!

If hypnotism is as defined, any fear we may have of it as being evil, then, is unfounded, for it is a *natural phenomena* of the human experience. It is the integral part of the learning process of the brain system; for if it were not naturally susceptible to suggestion, it could never learn any thing. And if our brain system was unable to learn anything, we would never get off of square one. So much for what hypnotism essentially is.

Now, let's take a brief look at what is involved while in a so-called hypnotic trance ...*concentration* of conscious attention. In the broad sense that our lives are directly influenced by the suggestiveness of our surroundings, our lives are even more so influenced by *purposeful suggestion* through hypnosis. Were you willing to allow yourself to be hypnotized, you would be *volunteering* yourself to participate in a controlled environment. While concentrating upon the suggestive words of the hypnotist your state of mind becomes altered to the point, that instead of relying upon the broad, independent gathering powers of all your senses, it *focuses* your hearing sensor upon the trusting words of the operator.

Were the operator to suggest your right arm is becoming numb and without feeling; that you are unable to feel pain even if he pricks it with a needle or cuts it with a knife, the suggestion will be impressed upon your brain system and processed just as takes place during an alert state. Were the operator to further suggest he is going to test the condition by sticking a needle in your arm ...with the assurance *you will feel nothing...* this information, too, will be dealt with as in any normal conscious state. Having ascertained there is no *threat* to your well-being because of the operator's assurance, you will feel *nothing,* the necessary physiological conditions will be carried out in accordance, and the operator can carry-out his test without inflicting pain to your arm; not because the hypnotist possesses occult powers, but because of the brain system's ability to bring about physiological changes in the body has always been a normal function of thought. Any time the Conscious' alertness to a threat of well-being can be subdued, either by hypnotic suggestion or self-imposed meditation, the brain system can, and will bring about *any* condition necessary *to comply with the data impressed upon it.*

A most remarkable example of this was revealed in an experiment carried out at Stanford University where a subject was hypnotized, placed in a room without food or water for 5 days, and told (suggested) he was in an orchard abundant with ripe fruit on its trees. For five days the subject took his nourishment from the *imaginary* fruit he picked from *imaginary* trees. At the end of the experiment he was examined by a team of doctors and found to be in the same degree of good health as when he began the experiment. This, by itself, is quite remarkable. But when it was discovered the subject had also gained weight ...as he might do from the type of fruit he was told to eat...the doctors were astounded!

Another example of the control your thoughts have over the physiological functions of your body is to tell a subject a specific spot on his forehead or arm is hotter than the rest of the skin surrounding it. By attaching a sensing device on the specific area, as well as the area around it, the change can be easily measured. It is not uncommon to find differences of several degrees in temperature between the spot and the surrounding area.

So-called feats of strength is another example of how thought will bring about the physical equivalent of a suggestion. Usually the smallest, frailest girl and the biggest, strongest athlete in the college classroom are asked to test their strength by squeezing a dynamometer. As suspected, at the outset the athlete far excels the timid squeeze of the young lady. Under hypnosis, however, told she can squeeze to a reading surpassing the best efforts of the athlete, she does so. ...with ease, and much to the chagrin of, guess who? So what about the common, every-day events involving thought?

AS YOU CHOOSE TO BELIEVE...

A friend I've known for some years, enjoying the challenge and satisfaction of playing a good game of golf before reaching her teens, entertained the thought of becoming a lady professional some day. Accepting the possibility in her memory and reinforcing (nurturing) it with dedicated practice, she became more and more proficient. As her proficiency grew, so did the prospect of seeing herself as a professional become more defined in her thoughts. It wasn't long before she found herself competing with the pros as a pro; not because of luck or chance, but because of the constructive thoughts she chose to plant and nurture in her mind. She's was just recently admitted to the LPGA Hall of Fame. Way to go Amy Alcott!

Another professional golfer, Steve Jones, winner of the 1989 Bob Hope Classic, praised Jesus Christ for his achievement. A man in California recently won 3 lotteries within a short period of time, attributing his success to a particular gold coin he possessed. Should the evening television inform you there's going to be another acute shortage of oil in this country shortly, you know what will happen? Right. Every one will rush out and fill up! Whether

Jesus, a gold coin or the TV had anything to do with it is really not the point. What is the point, is that "according to a person's thoughts, so it's going to be for *that* person."

Picture, if you will, yourself alone and walking down a mountain trail. Suddenly from out of nowhere a large, mean-looking grizzly-bear appears, growling and making-ready to charge you. How would this affect you? You would fear for your life, right? With this thought in mind, adrenaline would be released into your blood stream; your heartbeat would increase, your blood pressure would rise, your mouth would become dry, there would be ringing in your ears, your body would begin to tremble, and you'd probably soil your under pants ...a case of thought bringing about electro-biochemical changes in the body, i.e., "according to your thoughts, so it will be for you." Now what if you saw the same bear behind bars, would you have the same reaction? No, of course you wouldn't. Why? Obviously it isn't the bear, itself, that causes such reactions. It is, rather, the fear of what the bear could do to you under the circumstances; something you *choose* to think. So what if the bear you saw wasn't a bear at all, but rather an actor dressed-up in a bear costume? Does this tell you something about the magnitude of what can be produced by the thoughts we choose to dwell upon? Is it so difficult to understand that we act and behave, not according to what conditions actually are, but rather in accordance with what *we choose or allow* ourselves to believe them to be.

Most of us at some time or another have, out of necessity, been called upon to speak before an audience. Remember the sweaty palms, the dry throat, the slight empty feeling in your stomach, the nervousness and trembling body? What, really, is the difference between speaking before a crowd of strangers versus speaking to crowd of people you know? Nothing, really. But when we find ourselves the center of attention and lacking confidence, our imagination has a field day.

Before long we conjure up all sorts of negative thoughts; thoughts that we'll make mistakes, forget our lines, say something wrong, give a bad impression, receive unfavorable recognition, and so on. As a result, we find ourselves reacting to something that isn't a reality, but rather to a condition *we have created* in our memory system. In creating it we impose or imply a self-created *threat* to our social image ...and consequently, our brain system. Then, after evaluating the condition, our system responds to the *threat* accordingly: by causing us to be fearful. Thus, our actions become influenced, not by conditions as they actually are, but *as we imagine them to be!*

If someone were to place a heavy wooden plank on the ground and ask you to walk its length without falling off, you could probably do it with ease. If the same plank were placed several stories high between two buildings and you were asked to walk it, you probably couldn't do it. Why? Because of the *threat* of falling, of course. And it is because of this difference that we conjecture up thoughts of falling. But what about the steel workers who confidently walk the narrow beams and planks of high-rise buildings under construction, what's their story? Simple. They choose to believe in their ability to do so; they choose to concentrate their thoughts on what they are doing, not "what if?" Thoughts are things! They are as real to your system as any actual happening because any actuality *is so* to the degree that you *choose to believe it is.* By overcoming or negating fearful thoughts of falling with thoughts of confidence, anyone can carry-on in a normal manner hundreds of feet in the air or on the ground, because "what a person chooses to think, so it shall be for that person."

Speaking of "what if?", I'm reminded of the "great collapse" that took place in view of some 40 million golf enthusiasts around the country: the 1975 U. S. Open Golf

Championship ...a championship tournament where some of the finest golfers in the world mentally psyched themselves out of one of the richest prizes in golf.

What took place at the Medinah course number three on the 22nd of June is quite befitting and apropos to what we have been discussing: that as one chooses to think, so it will be for him or her.

Frank Beard, the third round leader, by his own admission, knew he had only to shoot a fourth round score of 74 on the last day to win all the marbles ...a score equivalent to his highest round in the tournament. He shot a 78 instead. Why?

Jack Nicklaus, probably the greatest golfer of all time, going into the 16th hole figured he had a lock on first place if he parred in ...something he could do any day of the week while wearing top hat and tails. He didn't though; he boggied each of the last three holes. Why?

Pressure, that's why. Not something caused by the other players; not something caused by a huge gallery; not something caused by a needed golf shot, but pressure caused by and inflicted upon oneself ...a case of mentally visualizing, feeling, experiencing a possibility of something that does not exist as a physical reality; something which is totally made up in the memory system ...an imagined possibility.

You could almost see the wheels turning in the leading players' heads. All were speculating, and all were dwelling upon a possibility of "what if" such and such should happen. And, of course, on the day of the "great collapse" it did, like clockwork. Six of the finest golfers in the world bit the dust because they couldn't control their thoughts.

True, every golfer who teed it up in the opening round of the tournament had a mental picture of himself winning the big one. But as each of the golfers' conscious fear of making a mistake was allowed to over-ride an otherwise subconscious execution of shot making, the objective formed by fearful thinking began to take its toll.

Lou Graham (the eventual winnner after a play-off the next day) came to the last hole in the final round leading the field by one shot. Having a simple 5 or 6 iron shot to the green ...the same kind of shot he has undoubtedly executed perfectly thousands of times before... hit it into a trap, came out short, missed the putt, necessitating a play-off the next day.

Every year thousands of pilgrims come to visit the famous Grotto of Lourdes, France, with the thought of being cured of some malady. Many are cured, as can be attested by the innumerable testimonials, empty wheel chairs, crutches, canes, braces, etc., left behind. Many people find this hard to accept. Why? If thought impressed upon the memory can bring about definite physiological changes in the body of someone thinking they've seen a bear that wasn't, why should it be any different for someone who chooses to believe that they can move a withered leg, accelerate the healing process or whatever regardless of what the diagnosis may show at the time? It isn't any different, because thought can bring about physiological results. Whatsoever a person chooses to believe, so it shall be for him or her.

When producing an educational drug film years ago, I had a special interest in photographing the Fire Walkers of Beqa in the Fiji Islands. I took shots of the bottom of their feet prior to and after the ceremony. The ceremony prior to the event involved about a 15-minute meditation period in a hut with the high priest. Then the Walkers came out and took their turns prancing around on rocks that had been heated for some 6-8 hours, reaching temperatures close to 1000 degrees! I personally tested the rocks, both by dropping a handkerchief amidst them, and standing on them momentarily. The handkerchief burst into flame immediately. And the bottom of my shoes were branded. As for the feet of the Fire Walkers? No change!

Most people would say it's impossible for a lady in her fifties, weighing less than 110 pounds to lift the rear of a heavy automobile off the ground, but according to ocassional newspaper articles it's happened a number of times, for a variety of reasons. In one case I'm familiar with, it happened because a grandmother was so overcome with the fear of her grandchild being crushed to death under the rear wheel of a car, she lifted the rear of it high enough so the child could be dragged to safety by another child standing-by.

Yogi Swami Rama, known for his experiences in manipulating his own physiologic responses, deliberately, consciously, and without moving a muscle, can cause the temperature of opposite sides of the palm of one hand to change in different directions achieving more than a 10 degree differential in an area less than two inches apart. He can also stop his heart and cause his ventricle to stand still for periods up to 20 seconds. How is it possible? Simply because Swami Rama *believes that it is possible.* And believing it makes it so to the "system" of Swami Rama!

In the article "Psychological Variables in Human Cancer," by Bruno Klopfer, in the Journal of Projective Techniques, Dr. Philip West related a most interesting story involving one of his patients:

Mr. Wright, his patient, had a generalized, far advanced malignancy involving the lymph nodes, lymphosarcoma. According to Dr. West, Wright developed resistance to all known palliative treatments, including X-rays and nitrogen mustard. Huge tumor masses the size of oranges were in the neck, axilles, groin, chest and abdomen. The spleen and liver were enormous. The thoracic duct was obstructed, and between one and two liters of milky fluid had to be drained from his chest every day. He was taking oxygen by mask frequently, and in the Dr's opinion was in a terminal state and untreatable.

In spite of this Mr. Wright was not without hope; the reason being that a drug he had heard about (Krebiozen, subsequently shown to be a useless, inert preparation) was coming on the market for testing. Although he wasn't qualified for testing, in that he had a prognosis of no more than two weeks, Wright persuaded his doctors to give him his chance at the "golden opportunity."

Receiving his first injection of the new drug on Friday, Dr. West didn't see Wright again until Monday. Having left him febrile, gasping for air, and completely bed-ridden, Dr. West found his patient walking around, chatting to the nurses and spreading his message of good cheer to anyone who would listen.

As for the status of the other patients involved in the testing, there was no change one way or another; only Wright had changed. His tumor masses had "melted like snow on a hot stove;" they were half their original size. According to Dr. West, this was phenomenal and demanded an explanation, "but not only that, it almost insisted that we open our minds to learn, rather than explain."

The injections were continued, and within 10 days, Wright was discharged from his "death-bed;" practically all signs of his disease having vanished in this short time. "Breathing normally and fully active, he took off in his plane and flew at 12,000 feet with no discomfort."

This unbelievable situation occurred at the beginning of the "Krebiozen" evaluation. But within two months conflicting reports began to appear in the news; the reports became more and more dismal, and Wright got wind of them.   As phenomenal as was his recovery, so was his relapse. Within weeks he was back in the hospital in much the same condition he was prior to taking the first injection.

Sensing an opportunity to double-check the drug and maybe, too, to find out how the quacks could accomplish the results they claimed, Dr. West took advantage of Wright's presence of mind by telling him not to believe what he had read in the papers; that the drug was really promising after all, and that he was expecting a shipment of a "new refined" double-strength dose of it any day while in reality, the Dr. planned to give him a placebo consisting of distilled water, and nothing more.

The results were even more astounding than those previous. Wright went back to flying and remained the picture of health, symptom free, for over two months, at which time the final AMA announcement appeared in the press: "Nation-wide tests show Krebiozen to be a worthless drug in the treatment of cancer." As to the affect this news had on Mr. Wright?   He was readmitted to the hospital soon after. "Lacking faith and hope, he succumbed in less than two days."

Along this same line, some years ago I heard from authoritative sources of a naval officer stationed at Camp Pendleton, California who went in for a medical check-up. After much testing he was sent to the Naval Hospital in San Diego for exploratory surgery.   It was found he had terminal cancer.   The doctors sewed him up and told him he had, at the outside, three months to live.   After receiving a medical discharge he took all his savings out of the bank and went to Europe for a last fling.   Friends of his working at the hospital, who had taken a "mind control" course, and wanting to help, decided to try an experiment while he was away. Synchronizing their thoughts three times a day, they "contemplated" a positive mental picture of their friend as they "chose" to see him ...in perfect health and like his old self.   About 6 weeks later the object of their thoughts appeared at the hospital looking better than ever.   The doctors familiar with the case couldn't believe what they were seeing. With his permission the doctors opened him up again and found that the cancer had not only been arrested, it was receding at an unbelievable rate. Asked by the doctors what he had done to bring about the change, the officer replied that he, himself, had done nothing, which was true, because he was totally unaware that others had been "thinking" him back to health.

Was this a fluke? No such thing. Phenomena, such as this, is happening every day, especially where constructive and purposeful thought is brought into play, either by the patient himself, or those who have the faith that thought, both positive and negative, inevitably produce the like of its kind, irrespective of who does the thinking, the time it is contemplated, or from where it originated.

Summation

So what can be concluded about the suggestive nature of thought? Simply this: As for thought, itself, it's powerful stuff, and when not properly controlled, it can get you into a lot of trouble ...as should be quite apparent when you consider what's going on in our society and the rest of the world today. As for it's suggestive nature, because of the enormity of successful accomplishments associated with it, hypnotic suggestion (self-suggestion) dramatically reveals two very important aspects about our brain system. One being, that potentially, each and every one of us has the capability of accomplishing far more than we have been led to believe. And the other is, that such a potential for accomplishment can be brought about through the simple application of *purposeful* thought. To be more specific, since the memory aspect of the brain system *does not,* and *cannot discern* itself with the nature of the data impressed upon it, and since all data impressed upon it is readily accepted as *factual* and in turn recorded as such in memory, it means that anyone on planet Earth, be they young folk, old folk, male, female, strong, weak, black, brown, red, yellow, green or purple, can purposely program their memory with the kind of data *they want it to have* with the assurance that at some point in time it will be carried out accordingly.   And so they can! As a matter of fact, every member of the human race has been doing just that all of their lives, but they haven't been doing it *purposely*. Unapprised of the true nature of their being and that their brain system is responsive to their thoughts, they've inadvertently allowed the suggestive nature of their immediate surroundings to do their "thinking" for them, so to speak. Such is the primary reason why so many people of the world are floundering in life as they are today. Out of their naive ignorance of their own greatness and ability to make things happen in their lives as they want them to be, they've inadvertently allowed those who do know such things to shape their lives for them, thus believing that their lot in life was meant to be. But hopefully, with what enlightenment I've provided you so far, you are at least aware that such is not the case; that with a little insight of self and purposeful thinking, *anyone* can change conditions in their life *as they want them to be!*

To reiterate the power of influence our thoughts have over the happenings we experience in our lives: We make (cause) things to happen in our lives ...good or bad... not so much because of who we are or the skill we employ, but rather because of the thoughts we allow to persist in our memory. And until the time comes when we can control our thinking to the point that we can block-out or overcome the possibility of adversity becoming a part of our lives, it will become a manifest condition; not because adversity is a necessary part of life, but because we allow it to become so as a result of our thinking that it can and does exist.

By now you should have a fair idea as to *who* you are and *why* you are what you are today. You should also have at least a hint as to the extent of what you can accomplish when you employ the use of purposeful thinking. Now it's time to turn to the *what* aspect of how you can change your life to be as you want it to become!

MENTAL IMAGERY

By imagination and reason we are able to turn experience into foresight; we become the creators of our future and cease to be the slaves of our past.

                                                                            Spenoza

I'm sure that few of us have cause to revel in the prospect that our lives are the inevitable result of an electro-biochemical brain system carrying-out its biological assignment in strict accordance with the data made available to it. And to even entertain the thought that our system is totally responsible for what we think, how we act, what we dream, what we want and desire, could, for some of us, be somewhat humiliating. But it is it. really? Think about it. Is it so humbling to discover that your *biological* brain system is preprogrammed by Nature to faithfully respond to whatever instructions *you wish* to give it, thus putting you in total control over your life? Is it so humiliating to know, with assurance, that the only thing that stands between you and making it "big" in life entails nothing more than making a few changes, here and there, in the nature of information of record in your *bio-chemical* memory? Hey, it doesn't get any better than this! What's to be humiliated about? It sure doesn't bother me. When I discovered the truth about my brain system years ago I was greatly relieved to find out that the way my life was going at the time had nothing to do with luck, chance, the breaks, God, or anything else of uncertainty or mystique, but was, rather, the inevitable result of my learning-machine-like brain system carrying-out its biological assignment in strict accordance with the data made available to it. What an eye opener! At last I had something concrete to go on. No more guess work. All I had to do to turn my life around entailed nothing more than learning to use my imagination with *purpose*. I did, and I haven't looked back since.

It's all so simple. Should you want to improve upon any condition in your life; making more money, developing a better skill, over-coming a tragedy or a drug problem, saving an unhappy marriage, eliminating bad habits,maintaining better health, what ever; by learning to utilize one's imagination in a *purposeful* way, anyone can impress their memory with the kind of data they want it to have and in turn alter their best interest and Self-Concept settings and in turn *compel* their brain system to achieve it accordingly. For example, let's suppose you're in the sales game and you're ill-at-ease around people. Why should you be ill-at-ease? Simply because you have a *prominence* of information in your memory that states that you're uncomfortable around people; the same information that is used by your Conscious in determining what's in your best interests and consequently directs you to think and behave accordingly. What's unfortunate about this is, not only will such thoughts and behavior cause you to suffer in sales as a consequence, but those same negative thoughts and behavior will be picked-up by your system's memory, thus reinforcing and providing additional prominence to what's already of record in memory!

So how does one bring this negative thinking and behavior to a halt and turn it around? Well, keeping in mind that any time you give conscious thought to something that you automatically bring your imagination into play, and that the imagined experience is faithfully recorded as *fact* and becomes a part of your memory, were you to *purposely* impress your memory with mental pictures stating the exact opposite ...that you were very much at ease with people, this experience too, like any other sensory experience, will become a part of memory. In doing so, it will have the affect of partially *diluting* the prominence of the negative data in memory representing you're uneasiness around people. And were you to continue to purposely impress your memory with these positive thoughts, there would soon come a time when there would be more data of record in your memory indicating that *you are* comfortable around people than there would be that you *were not* comfortable. Once this stage is reached, that learning-machine brain system of yours would have no other choice than to respond accordingly by causing you to feel comfortable around people. Even more rewarding, once you effected such a change in attitude, there would come still more constructive changes: You would experience an increase in sales, your bank account would grow, you would make new friends, and so on, the experiences of which, in turn, would be impressed upon your memory and consequently further reinforce those positive experiences which you had previously impressed upon it in the first place. In other words, once you start impressing your memory with positive and constructive data, your brain system will eventually begin to *output* comparable results, which in turn become automatically impressed upon your memory and, as a consequence, further reinforce the data which was input initially, causing your brain system to further output even more-so positive results, ad infinitum.

Now I realize there are some of you, perhaps, who feel it is wrong to purposely deceive your brain system by impressing it with so-called "false data." But is it, really? Is it so wrong to imagine yourself doing or becoming something you're potentially and quite capable of achieving? Is it false to state the truth? To the contrary, it's totally deceitful to waste your life doing less than you're potential and capabilities demand based upon what's been learned from hypnotism. Not only is it wrong, it is an utter waste of human talent! Remember what the Bible had to say about talent? *For a man who has something and uses it will have more. But for the man that has something and doesn't use it ...he shall lose it and have nothing.* (Matt. 25:29).

There was also a passage pertaining to "purposeful" suggestion: *...when you pray you should believe the condition already exists as you want it to be ...and it will come unto you.* (Mark 11:24).

No, I don't believe it's the least bit wrong to intentionally deceive your brain system by suggesting that a condition of your choice already exists. After all, in light of the fact we have the potential and capability to achieve far greater than what our past experiences have led us to believe, who or what is deceiving whom?

STATEMENT

Do you know what an affirmation is? For those who don't, an affirmation is an allegation, a declaration, a confirmation of anything established *...a statement of belief.*

Whether you know it or not, you have been making affirmations just about every moment of your wakeful life. For example, do you have any idea how many times you have mentally pictured, mentally felt, and mentally verbalized concepts such as: "I can't!" ..."Monday is a lousy day of the week!" ..."I'm unlucky!" ..."I'll never get..." ..."It's impossible!" You've been making such affirmations most of your life. We all have. And chances are, most of your Mondays turned out to be lousy, and it turned out you were unlucky, and it was impossible for you, and you never did get whatever it was you didn't think you'd get.

Without realizing it, in making such innocent(?) heretofore-thought statements, even though you may think you didn't actually believe in what you were thinking (affirming) at the time, the fact that you impressed your memory with such negativism, it was, and always will be, accepted by your system and made a part of memory just as is the case with any other happening sensed by one your receptors. And, as with any other happening, the data defining the experience will be taken into account in all decision-making done by your Conscious.   With a Conscious continually being influenced by such data, is it any wonder why people can't do that certain something, or why their performance on Monday is not up to par with the other days of the week? How could it be otherwise? Data is data, no matter how you cut it. There's no such thing as your memory discriminating between what is good or bad data. All data impressed upon the memory is accepted *as is*. If the data happens to be negative, it's going to produce negative results (as in computerese: garbage in, garbage out). The same is true for positive data. It's all so simple: whatsoever you input ...purposely or otherwise... your memory accepts "as is" and your Conscious must deal with it ...negatively or positively... accordingly. It has always been that way; it is the nature of your biological programmed brain system; it will never change!

Now, should you question the fact that such negative statements have a profound affect upon your Conscious consider, if you will, what's involved: When you make an off-the-cuff statement, such as "I can't," do you utter words only, or do you utter the words while at the same time reflect upon a mental picture depicting some past experience of failure? And don't forget the reference to Mondays, either; don't you mentally reflect upon past Mondays as being different from other days of the week? Sure you do. It's near impossible to give conscious thought to something and not associate it with some past experience because it is *your past experiences that give rise to your thoughts in the first place.* You form a mental picture of what you're going to eat for breakfast before preparing it; you form mental pictures of what you're going to do while driving to work; you plan a vacation by mentally picturing what you're going to see and do; and when you step up to strike a golf ball you have a mentally picture what the ball's going to do before you execute the shot. So what do you think happens to all this mental imagery of lousy Mondays, that "you can't", and so on? Do you think it's like so much smoke up the chimney? Not on your life! Even smoke up the chimney affects someone or some thing. The experience of mental imagery is as real to your brain system as any other form of experience; it, like every causative action, produces an effect, and every effect in turn produces another causative action. Mental pictures formed in your brain are an effect produced by the causative action of data pertaining to past experiences.   The effect produced, in turn, causatively affects the Conscious to process the effect, whereupon the effect becomes a part of memory that will causatively effect some thought in the future, and so on, ad infinitum.

The key thing to remember here is, that thought ...any thought... is a *memorable* experience to your system. And should you doubt it, you can prove it to yourself by reaching back into your memory and try to recall a story or some joke you heard. In doing so, what is your recall? Does just the story line come to mind, or do you recall both the words and pictures you mentally formulated in response to the descriptive words impressed upon your memory by the teller? Obviously, your recall reflects the whole experience, doesn't it? Certainly it does, because all conscious recall is related in the form of mental pictures; pictures imagined or otherwise ...which brings to mind an experience had by a dear friend of mine from London, England. During his visit here in the States some years ago, he underwent a traumatic experience of hallucinating ...later diagnosed as a reaction caused by a combination of drugs prescribed by his doctor. When I say traumatic, it really was! For several days he was imagining hands coming out of plastered walls, cobwebs encircling him, little people trying to steal his belongings. He even carried on a conversation with his dead sister of ten years past. The last morning, before I placed him in a hospital, I found him in his room huddled up in the back of a clothes closet fearfully yelling for me to hide because of some imagined gangsters that were trying to kill the two of us. Not only was he near panic, he was short of breath and sweating profusely. And do you know what? Even to the day shortly before his demise ...keeping in mind his experiences were fantasized... he had total recall of it, down to the finest detail! Keeping in mind his recall was based upon fantasized experiences ...not actual happenings in the real sense of the words, I ask you: do the experiences expressed by mental imagery become a permanent part of memory and produce effects accordingly? You can bet the farm on it! And because the memory does not, and cannot, discern itself with the nature of the experiences impressed upon it ...the possibility of whether or not hands can reach out from plastered walls or that you can't do something in particular, that Mondays are a drag... there's no reason whatsoever to believe your memory won't accept purposely impressed mental pictures of how you would like to see yourself becoming or accomplishing, either.

Okay. If you can accept the fact that the only source of data available to your brain system is that which your memory receives from its sensors; that once received your memory does not, and cannot, discern itself between what is an imagined experience and what is actual, and that your Conscious carries out its functions in terms of your thoughts and behavior in direct accordance with this data, we can now remove your practice of indiscriminate mental imagery from the haphazard realm and turn it into a useful tool in programming your memory with the kind of information you *want it to have.*

DATA NEGATING

By now, you should know that the only thing preventing you from doing or becoming whatever you desire in life is either due to the lack of, or the presence of, specific constructive or restrictive data of record in your memory. And you should also know, that even though your memory may presently contain certain restrictive or unwanted data which cannot be removed or erased, *it can be displaced* by inputting *contrary* data of your own choosing.

As to how this condition can be brought about, imagine, if you will, a brim-full bucket of water and a pile of pebbles stacked next to it. For purposes of illustration, consider the water as representing the unwanted negative and restrictive data of record in your memory, and the pebbles representing the positive and constructive data you wish to impress upon it Now, in the sense that you take a pebble from the pile, drop it into the bucket and displace an equivalent amount of water, so is the equivalent of restrictive data *displaced* in your memory when you impress it with a single bit of data representing how you want things to be. Obviously, a single bit of constructive data impressed upon your memory is not going to turn the tide anymore than a single pebble is going to displace all the water in the bucket. But it's a start! As the saying goes: even the longest of journeys begins with the first step.

Now what if you made a practice of impressing your memory with constructive bits of data? Like dropping one pebble after another in the bucket, after a period of time it would conceivably reach a point that the bucket contained one-half restrictive data and one-half constructive data. When such a point is reached, what sort of an affect do you think this would have upon the decision-making of your Conscious? At least, it would be a toss-up ...a south-of-the-border stand-off... wouldn't it? So what if you continued impressing your memory with additional constructive data, what then? Eventually there would be a greater volume of constructive data in memory than restrictive. Right? It would also mean, that in displacing the restrictive data, the new constructive data would become the dominant influence insofar as defining your best interests and Self-Concept. It would mean, that in displacing unwanted data with data of your choice, you would be in conscious control of your brain system. And once in control of your system you would, by virtue of calling your own shots, be in the driver's seat; you would be in the position to program your system to make things happen in your life just as you wanted them to be!

PEBBLES TO BOULDERS

After many years of ignorance and neglect as to the affect your surroundings have been having upon you, it is reasonable to assume that vast amounts of restrictive data have undoubtedly found their way into your memory. It is also reasonable to assume it would take some doing trying to negate it in a reasonable period of time on the basis of one pebble at a time. Is there a way to speed up the data displacement process? Fortunately, there is, and it has to do with prominence.

Remember prominence? Earlier we spoke of two ways to bring it about. One is by *repetition* ...that of repeatedly impressing the memory with the same information; the equivalent of dropping single pebbles one-at-a-time into the bucket. The other was by *emotional association* ...the equivalent of dropping a single *rock* in the bucket? Well, there is yet still another method; that of *detail* ...having the equivalence of a *boulder!*

Obviously, if one is in a hurry to negate unwanted data in the memory, incorporating the use of *detail* and *emotion* is going to get the job done much faster than by *repetition* alone. Assuming this to be the case with you, then any programming you plan to do in the future should consist of specifically defining what it is you wish to change, forming a mental picture that best expresses it, and adding detail and emotion to the same degree as that which you would experience had the desired change already taken place (Mark 11:24). For example, suppose you wanted to improve your shot-making in golf. The first thing you would do after having considered specific points you wish to improve on, is to commence your mental imagery incorporating a golf course most familiar to you. This being the setting, you would then begin adding detail ...prevailing wind, angle of the sun, sounds of other golfers on adjacent fairways, etc. Once the setting was established in your memory, you would then bring yourself into the picture wearing your favorite golfing attire. Included in this picture you would note your golf bag, the clubs in it, and your favorite caddie handing you a club as you step-up to the tee and execute a perfect shot down the middle of the fairway. You would then shift the picture from seeing yourself (externalizing) to that of "feeling" or becoming yourself, in that you would begin picturing ...both perceptually and emotionally ...the "feeling" of how well you have been striking the ball; the fact that you are only one over par; that the shot you just executed is in perfect position for a possible birdie, etc. "Feeling" yourself arriving at the ball you just drove perfectly, you would imagine the feeling of taking a club, making a practice swing, then addressing the ball, striking it, and watching it arch toward the pin on the green ...all the time mentally seeing and feeling like it was actually happening.

Obviously, a mental picture of this magnitude is going to have a much greater impact on your memory than something casual and vague. It's the difference between using boulders and pebbles. And just as obvious, when you think in terms of boulders you're going to produce a greater degree of prominence in a much shorter time than you would with just pebbles.

To give you an idea of the effect and rate of improvement possible by such detailed and emotionalized mental imagery, according to an article written-up in the Research Quarterly Magazine some years ago, a group of students conducted an experiment in the use of mental imagery to improve their skills. They were divided into three groups and were to practice "free throws" with a basketball. Each of the groups were tested as to their proficiency prior to the experiment as well as at its conclusion. Group One was told to practice free-throws for twenty minutes a day over a period of twenty days. Group Two was told not to touch a basketball at all during the twenty-day period. Group Three was told to practice for the same amount of time as Group One, but to do it mentally and without touching a ball.

At the conclusion of the experiment, Group One, which had actually been the only group to practice with a ball, showed an improvement of 24%. Group Two obviously showed no improvement at all; their proficiency was less than at the beginning of the test. As for Group Three, despite the fact they had not had a basketball in their hands during the test period, they showed an improvement of 23%!

The use of mental imagery brings about positive results whenever it's used. Alekhine, an obscure chess player at the time, used mental imagery to beat the world famous Capablana in a championship match ...the result, he claimed, of "mentally practicing chess in his mind for three months before the match."

World famous pianist Arturo Schnabel was quoted as saying he prefers to practice in his head as opposed to practicing at length on the piano.

Ben Hogan, one of the world's greatest golfers, used mental imagery before each shot. He said he "feels" the club head on the ball "in his imagination" before he steps up and actually strikes it.

Another great golfer, Gary Player, used to stand in front of a mirror early in his career and affirm, "I'm going to be the greatest golfer in the world! I'm going to be the greatest golfer in the world!" He must have said it fifty times at a sitting, according to his teacher, Phil Ritson. For my money Gary Player *is* one of the greatest golfers in the world. He's also a great gentlemen!

In the Winter Olympics, perhaps you've noticed how the top slalom and downhill racers use mental imagery of themselves skiing the course just prior to leaving the gate? Ask any top athlete; they all use mental imagery to assist them in their particular event.

Summation

As for the conclusions we can draw from all of this: *We are what we are at this moment as a result of what we have experienced in the past.* And unless we change the substance of our past experiences, there's little reason for us to expect our future lives to be any different from what they are at present. The question then, is can we change the substance of our past experiences. Unfortunately, the answer is no. What you've experienced in the past will remain with you throughout your lifetime. But it is well within your capability to over-come or displace past experiences with those of your own choosing, and subsequently cause your Conscious to direct you accordingly.

What is needed then, is a plan.

PLANNING FOR TOMORROW

Whatsoever can be inwardly conceived can be outwardly experienced.

Might I say at this point, since I have guaranteed that you can make anything happen in your life as you want it to be ...including making a lot of money, if that's what you wish. I am well aware of your possible eagerness to start "making it" and bringing materialistic prosperity into your life. It is for this reason I wish to caution you about skipping over the material we are about to cover here. In my mind, there is no objective you cannot attain. But should you attempt to achieve it without properly preparing for it, you would be both foolish and unwise. And as far as I know, the only endeavor in which you start at the top is digging a hole! For this reason, then, it is suggested that any plan for the future be developed in such a way that you be totally prepared to receive that which is awaiting you. Such a plan, as I see it, should be incorporated into two steps: that of *personal* goals, and *materialistic* goals. The reason for this is simple: Although there is no clear differentiation in the method of their attainment, there are certain psychological factors involved which suggest that once you have your personal goals in order, you are not only better prepared to receive you materialistic goals, but that you will find them that much easier to attain, as well. With this in mind we'll proceed.

As I see it, there are only two reasons people fail to realize their true potential and capability. One is, that most people don't realize the extent of their potential and capability. And the other is, being aware of it but not knowing how to put it to use.

By now you should know that insofar as your potential and capability to make things happen in your life as you want them to be is no different than anyone else's; that because of the innate genetic ensembles that are part of our systems, every human being possesses the potential and capability to achieve whatsoever has been achieved by those before them. This being the case, it becomes a simple matter, then, of learning how to put your potential and capability to use. For that you need a plan. A plan by itself is useless, however, unless it can be properly carried-out. And in order to do so, you're going to have to be prepared; you need to prepare yourselves in matters that count, primarily those pertaining to Self, Family and Business or occupation. These are the areas where improvement is absolutely essential if you ever expect to successfully make it big in material attainment.

It is a fact, that were you to improve only in the category of Self, the results of it would be reflected throughout the other phases of you life as well. But that alone is not enough for the kind of success we're talking about; you want to possess the element of success for every phase of your life: specifically, in your family life and business or occupation as well, then you will have three categories of success that are constantly working to uphold you on top of outstanding success. The reason for this is simple. There are a number of people who have "made it" successfully in business, which, of course, makes it possible for them to enjoy materialistic success. But when it comes to being successful as a person and family-wise, they are generally absolute failures. And because they are failures, the enjoyment they should experience from their material success never seems to materialize in the other categories. Material success means very little if you are a miserable person to be associated with and there's no one to share your success with. So, for true happiness in all phases of your life, your plan should include becoming successful in all categories. Okay?

THE MOTIVATING FORCE

In an attempt to become successful there is no doubt that each of us could stand some improvement in a number of things. But nothing is so important to the attainment of personal success as that of knowing how to attract and get along with people, for it is solely because of people that it is possible for you to not only become successful, but once attained, to have full appreciation of possessing it, as well. Successfully dealing with people is the essence of what life is all about. Without peoples' support, their affection and cooperation, there is little meaning to life. People should be as important to you as you are to yourself. So if you want to get the most out of life, you must learn to attract and deal with people successfully.

So how do you attract and deal successfully with people? It's really quite simple: you give them what they want the most! And what do people want the most? Ask yourself. No, it's not money. No, it's not success. And no, it's not peace-of-mind. What you and every other person in the world really want the most, aside from survival, is *recognition* and *appreciation*.

This desire for recognition and appreciation is as innate to our being as life itself. It is the basic motivating force behind everything we think and do. In some cases it is even more important than survival! It is responsible for the friends we keep, the things we do for others, the style of clothes we wear, the kind of car we drive, the establishments we patronize, the home we purchase, and so on. And contrary to what most people think, the recognition and appreciation we so insatiably strive for throughout our lives can never be found by trying to impress others with reference to our own importance, because in doing so we commit the most unpardonable of sins: we inadvertently point out to others how lesser-important they are compared to us. Any time you feel like you want to "turn people off" fast just tell them how great you are ...inadvertently, or otherwise.

When you turn people off, you not only discourage them from wanting to be your friend, to support and help you, you also deny yourself of any hope of them showing appreciation for you, which is the very reason we feel inclined to impress people with our importance in the first place.   Crazy, isn't it? What it all adds up to is this: If you wish to satisfy your desire for recognition and appreciation (which we all innately do), you must always make sure you give it to the other person first. This is *the* basic tenet in dealing with people successfully. Give *recognition* and *appreciation* to others to the same degree you seek it, and they will reciprocate in spades!

It's not your appearance, it's not the car you drive, it's not how much money you have, and it's not the kind of home you live in that impresses others *the most*. What impresses people the most is someone *who shows them the recognition and appreciation they are seeking!* Making people feel recognized and appreciated not only assures you of their friendship and cooperation, it also "turns them on" to the point that they feel compelled to reciprocate even more so ...an integral part of what being successful is all about, whether it be on a personal basis, a family relationship, or conducting business.

As you know, "consciously" trying to show appreciation toward someone you "think" you don't like is not easy. It will be, however, once you've instructed your *memory* in terms of what "turns people on." Before you know it, and without any conscious effort, shortly after you begin programming your memory with the kind of information you want it to have, the reality of it will become so natural in your daily experiences you won't even be aware of it. As a matter of fact, as a result of programming your memory, your whole way of life will change dramatically. When you meet new people or associate with past acquaintances, you'll find thoughts of like and dislike almost non-existent; you'll just naturally find yourself genuinely interested in them because of the fact that you've programmed yourself to appreciate people for what they are They, of course, will respond with enthusiasm, which will "turn you on." Subsequently, because of their enthusiastic response, *your* desire for recognition and appreciation will be satisfied. Before long you'll discover that having a good relationship with people ...strangers, friends, acquaintances... is what life is all about! ...at least so it has been for me. Like successfully dealing with everything else is life, dealing with people is nothing but a case of invoking the principle of Cause and Effect: *cause* others to be recognized and appreciated and they will *effect* recognition and appreciation upon you. When you can manage this, you will become successful in whatever you do.

Now for the plan. You will need some paper and pencil. Try to pick a time when you are wide-awake, and slip-off to some quiet place where you won't be disturbed for an hour or so. Ready? Take a sheet of paper and across the top print S E L F in large letters.

S E L F

The primary objective of the Self category is for you to become a very desirable and pleasing person to be around; keeping in mind, of course, nobody ever gets a second chance to make a first impression.

As you undoubtedly know, whatever we do in this world considered worthwhile, regardless of what it may be, involves other people. Before you can ever expect to get their assistance in helping you along your way, however, it is necessary that you cause them to be attracted to you. This is easily done when you make it a point to always greet people with a an inviting, friendly *smile*. So in the upper left hand

corner of the sheet of paper in front of you, print the word
CAUSE. After "cause," print the word, SMILE. Just below
the word, "cause," print the word, EFFECT. After "effect,"
you should write a brief account of *why* you want to smile,
and the result you should expect from doing it. For example,
you might write: "I want to smile because it informs people I
wish to be friendly."

Just below the word, "effect," print the word,
AFFIRMATION. After "affirmation," you should make an
affirmative statement about the characteristic of smiling;
stating the condition as you want it to be. For example, you
could write "I ALWAYS WEAR A SMILE!" Note the way in
which the affirmation is stated; it doesn't infer that you are
going to smile at some future date, the inference is that you
always wear a smile! So write it that way!

Perhaps at this point it should be mentioned just what it is
we are attempting to do. Affirmations are the "guts" of your
plan. How they are written, and in turn, interpreted by your
Conscious, has everything to do with the effectiveness of your
plan. For instance, were you to write the statement, "I am
going to start wearing a smile," your Conscious could
interpret this to mean it shouldn't cause you to smile until
that time occurs.

SELF

1. CAUSE: Smile

    EFFECT: "I want to smile because it informs people
             I wish to be friendly."

    AFFIRMATION: "I always wear a smile!"

The inference that you are "going to" is a negative
connotation, making it that much tougher to overcome if you

aren't presently smiling. Besides, your Conscious might have it's own interpretation of when "going to" should take place. With no specific date to work with, your Conscious has no reason to bring about any condition until it decides to do so ...which could be never!

When writing affirmations, they should always be stated in the present tense with the inference that they do, in fact, already exist. In this way, once the influence of such data reaches the point that it overcomes the data in memory presently preventing it from happening, your Conscious will have to respond accordingly ...as you stated it to be... now!

Should you be wondering if writing out all of this cause, effect, and affirmation stuff is really necessary, the answer is: Absolutely! Affirmative! Yes! Probably for the first time in your life you will be clearly defining to your memory just what it is you want your system to accomplish for you.

Possibly you might think that because you already consider smiling as being essential in attracting people that it's not necessary to make a big deal about it. Perhaps it isn't if such is the case. But unless you're wearing a smile all the time, the data in your memory isn't prominent enough.

Prominence of data in memory is the name of the game! And the only way to insure that certain data becomes prominent enough to bring about comparable results is to plan and program for it. Nothing should be overlooked! For instance, when you print "cause," followed by the word "smile," a certain amount of prominence is brought about in your memory just by doing it because it has been clearly defined to your Conscious that a smile is definitely the "cause" responsible for attracting others. And when you write "effect," followed by a statement of your feelings as to how things should turn out, you are adding still further prominence to what you're trying to accomplish. In one respect you are providing your Conscious justification for smiling, and for another, by telling it what the results will be beforehand, once realized the experience of it happening will further reinforce the causative affirmative statement, thus making it more credible and helpful in assuring its attainment of prominence.

As said before, you should never assume anything insofar as your Conscious is concerned. Writing out a plan, verbally voicing an affirmation, calling your imagination into play ...all are experiences to your memory, and subsequently become of record in your memory. Whether purposely directed to your memory or not, it faithfully records everything that you think and do. And the more clearly the experience is expressed, the greater the impression it has on your memory You are, in a sense, communicating with a mechanism. And when dealing with such, it will carry out its function exactly as instructed ...in accordance with the information made available to it.

Continuing with the plan... once you have been fortunate enough to attract people to you, you should attempt to keep them around. This can be easily accomplished if you will give them your full attention. You can do this by *showing a sincere interest in people!* So, just under all that has been written on "smiling," print CAUSE. After "cause", write, "Showing an interest in people." As you did before, under the heading of "cause," print EFFECT. After "effect" write a statement of why you want to be interested in other people. For example, you might write: "By showing a sincere and genuine interest in people I won't be monopolizing the conversation. Thus, I'll make them feel important and they'll show their appreciation in return." And while we're on the subject, one of the most effective ways of showing other people you're really interested in them, is their first impression of how you shake hands. Is it limp? Or is it enthusiastic? Go for a firm hand shake. It tells it all. Better yet, use both hands; one shaking, and the other clasped around their wrist or forearm. That's the clincher. Politicians have been using that move for centuries in order to sway a potential voter that he/she is sincerely interested in their best interests.

Again, as before, print the word, AFFIRMATION under the word, "effect," and write out a simple statement of belief, such as, "I ALWAYS SHOW A SINCERE INTEREST IN OTHER PEOPLE!"

Because other people have been attracted to you and you have momentarily held their interest by seemingly showing a sincere interest in them, you must reinforce this impression by convincing them you mean business. You can do it by *encouraging them to talk about themselves* (which they'll be delighted to do). Besides, by encouraging them to talk about themselves, you won't be tempted to talk about yourself and possibly turn them off. So under the heading of "sincere interest in other people," print the word, CAUSE. After "cause" write, "Encourage others to talk about themselves." Below the word, "cause," print the word, EFFECT, followed by a statement of why it is important to encourage others to talk about themselves. Under the word, "effect," print the word, AFFIRMATION. After "affirmation" you should write something like this: "I ALWAYS ENCOURAGE OTHERS TO TALK ABOUT THEMSELVES!"

Since having people appreciate you is going to become one of your greatest assets, it would be smart to give them something even more to be impressed with. Nothing is more pleasing to people ...including yourself... than hearing the sound of their name being spoken by another person. As before, write out a descriptive statement after the word, "cause," followed by the word, "effect," and a statement as to why it's important to call people by name. When it comes to the affirmation, write it as follows: "I ALWAYS REMEMBER PEOPLES' NAMES AND FACES!" But it's always been hard for me to remember peoples' names, you might be thinking. Forget it! That may be the case today, but it won't be in the near future. It should be remembered that you are making a statement to a learning machine (your brain) that readily accepts whatever you wish to impress upon it. Just give it the data, and your brain system will find a way to transform the suggestion (affirmation) into a reality. And you don't have to force the data on your memory, either. Any time the use of force or effort is brought into play when dealing with the brain, it implies doubt; it's like saying "I have doubts this affirmation stuff will work, so I'd better try harder." A word of caution: always avoid the use of effort and force when dealing with your brain system. Be gentle, instead. Impress data upon your memory with the same sort of assurance and confidence you employ in the things you know you do well.

I don't know about you, but I, personally, enjoy being around a person who exudes enthusiasm much more than one who doesn't. I mean, it's nice to be around someone who smiles, shows a sincere interest in me and what I have to say, who encourages me to talk about myself and remembers and calls me by name. But when they do all of these things with enthusiasm it really "turns me on;" it seems to verify that all the other things are not "put-on." How about you, don't you agree? If you do, I strongly suggest you put this one on the list, also. For the affirmation, make it: "I ALWAYS SHOW AN ENTHUSIASTIC ATTITUDE ABOUT EVERYTHING I DO!"

One way of lousing-up a good on-going relationship is by becoming involved in an argument. Providing you have employed the first five characteristics correctly, you should have no trouble keeping people interested in you. As long as it remains that way they will more than likely prove helpful in the fulfillment of your future plans for success. Argue with them, however, tell them they are wrong, and you can kiss 'em good-bye. No one ever wins an argument no matter how right they are. Avoid any kind of misunderstanding much as you would AIDS! So that it can be properly seated in your memory, write this characteristic down as you did the others and finish it off with the following affirmation: "I ALWAYS RESPECT THE OTHER PERSON'S OPINION!"

Okay. At this point, if you have done as instructed, you should have a list of affirmations as follows:

1. I always wear a smile!

2. I always show a sincere interest in other people!

3. I always encourage others to talk about themselves!

4. I always remember peoples' names and faces!

5. I always show an enthusiastic attitude about every thing I do!

6. I always respect the other person's opinion!

When you have successfully displaced much of the restrictive data that is presently keeping you from acting in accordance with what you have just written, you will be pleasantly surprised to find few, if any, people dislike you; that they genuinely enjoy your presence. You will also be well on your way to becoming one of the nicest persons you know. People will be attracted to you because you have learned to give them what they want most: the recognition and appreciation they innately seek.

As you know, "consciously" trying to show appreciation toward someone you "think" you don't like is not easy. It will become so, however, once you've instructed your memory in terms of what "turns people on." In the meantime, tell you what, here's a little game you can play that can be rewarding to both you and the subject. I've been doing it for years In addition to the programming you'll be doing shortly, starting right now, make a conscious effort to turn people on that you meet for the first time ...maybe someone at the local bar, the mechanic working on your car, or someone at the lunch counter. Begin the game with a nice smile. Make them feel like you're delighted to be in their presence. Now get them to talk in terms of their interests (usually themselves). Ask for their name, then use it profusely! Pour on the recognition they're seeking by complimenting them whenever possible. Then when they inquire about you, briefly tell them what they want to know, then *switch* the conversation back to them. The reward is in knowing *you're in control* as you continue to put the ball in their court. In doing so, not only will you make them feel good about having met you, you'll also come away with good thoughts about yourself. It's a nice feeling! Try it. First thing you know, it will become a gratifying habit.

FAMILY

Now what about your family life? Do you have any bad habits? Are you attentive to what others have to say? Are you giving members of the family the appreciation they are seeking? Do you contribute your share to family life? How about your manners? Is your personal-hygiene impeccable? This is an area that can only be explored by you. If you will take the time to "sneak" a long, hard look at yourself, I'm sure you can come-up with at least five characteristics that could be improved upon. Add them to the list just as you did the previous characteristics.

BUSINESS

What about your job, are you putting forth your best for your employer? Do you take an extra long coffee break? Do you do more than is expected of you? Are you aware that insofar as outsiders are concerned, the integrity of the company you work for *is judged on the basis of their first impression of you?*

Assuming you wish to be successful in work or business, there are five essential characteristics you should program for. The first of these is that of being *aggressive*. Whether you are self-employed or employed by others; whether your job is on the outside or you are chained to a desk, the person who is aggressive and enterprising in doing his or her job will be doing it far better than one who is not. To be aggressive does not mean you are to over-step your bounds by walking over your fellow employees or chase customers down the street, however. As used here, it simply means you should attack your job with the degree of enthusiasm you would employ in playing your favorite sport or game; you should enjoy what you are doing and play at it to win.

As a kid, right out of college, I went to work for a large corporation. I lasted for about three months, and I'll tell you why: I was considered aggressive. To my amazement, I was called on the carpet for being too aggressive. I was told to adapt my working hours to that of accomplishing a certain amount of work ...no more, and no less. It was also inferred that by not doing it I would upset the balance of the whole system. Trying to look busy was not my cup-of-tea, so I left and have been self-employed ever since. If you run into the same, I strongly suggest you find something better, also. You are too good for those who don't appreciate employees who enjoy their work and play to win. Besides, with such an attitude, what sort of opportunity for success do you think there would be open to you working for such a company? Move on! There are too many companies dying to get their hands on someone who is aggressive.

As before, after the numeral follow with the word, CAUSE. After "cause" write the word, AGGRESSIVE. Below "cause" print EFFECT. After "effect" write a statement as to why it is important to be aggressive in business. Your reason could be: "I want to be aggressive because I will be doing more than is expected of me, which in turn will help me to stand-out as a valuable asset to the person or company I work for."

Your affirmation should be written as follows: "I AM ALWAYS AGGRESSIVE IN EVERYTHING I DO!" Again, I repeat: employers love enterprising employees, but not the ones who step on the toes of others. Be aggressive, but not at the expense of someone else!

How's your *confidence?* Do you know your job or product well enough to convince others you do? This is an area in business that is most essential. Having and conveying confidence in what you're doing means everything! A person who doesn't evade, side-step or make excuses, but rather speaks and acts with assurance, is the person who makes the sale or gets the job done successfully. With confidence behind your every thought and action, you become an expert in the eyes of those dealing with you. People prefer to deal with experts. And if you happen to be in sales, it's a sure bet you have sold yourself as an expert before the sale is made. If you're a little shaky on your product, at least give the impression of confidence; that is the first thing the customer looks to. As before, make your affirmation a positive statement, i.e., "I AM ALWAYS CONFIDENT ABOUT EVERYTHING I DO!"

Do you become discouraged when things don't work out for you? Are you looking for an easy way out? Don't be! Be *persistent!* Stick to what you have set out to do. Play at your job as you would work at competing in your favorite sport. Be persistent in your endeavor to win. Like any sport ... fishing, golf, tennis, etc... each represents a different challenge to different people. In such endeavors most of us fall short of what we want to accomplish; we are never completely satisfied, but it doesn't keep us from trying it over and over again. Play at your job in the same vein. Strive for excellence. Be persistent! Persistence, like procrastination, can become a habit in life; the former takes just a little more of an endeavor than the latter. Whatever form of endeavor is applied toward today's achievements becomes a habit of *ease* tomorrow. Put PERSISTENCE down on your list as you have done the others.

Are you always on time at the job or when you make an appointment? Do you see that the goods are delivered as promised? Do you excuse yourself from idle conversation to wait on a customer? Are you *reliable* at what you do?

When I used to employ a gang of carpenters while in the construction business, I had one man who was much older than the rest. He was not very aggressive, nor did he display much confidence, but he was always on the job on time. You could set your watch by his reliability. For that he was a tremendous asset. Employers can usually excuse a man who lacks the other characteristics mentioned, but when an employee is not dependable, he is at the same time undesirable. Whenever you set a time and place involving others, you are demanding of them to be there; you are asking for both time and effort. If you are unreliable and fail to fulfill your obligation with them, you are literally robbing them of materialistic value, namely money, because time and effort is money.

Write this one down like the others. You should have lots of reasons why it's important to be a reliable person. Your affirmation should be: "I AM RELIABLE IN EVERYTHING I DO!"

There is nothing that will get you ahead faster in any kind of business than that of being *creative*. There is always a better way to get things done on the job or in business. There is always a need for improvement. Through creativity, products can be made available to the public costing less and made better. Time, which means money, can be saved through certain creative thinking. Things can be done more efficiently through creative thinking. Clients have saved millions due to the creative thinking of some sharp accountant, attorney or investment counselor. Many companies offer bonuses to those who come-up with ways to save money. Writers make a better living being creative. Inventors depend upon their creativeness. Even the kid selling newspapers on the corner can become successful by thinking creatively. The same is true of the housewife, the fisherman, secretary, laborer, postman, etc. Thinking creatively is very important in any line of endeavor. There is always a better way of doing things. Someone is going to come-up with a better approach to something, so why not make it you? You have a brain system that will find creative solutions to any problem presented it. Program it to be creative, and you'll be surprised with what it comes up with. Put CREATIVE down on your list just like the others. Your affirmation should be: "I AM A CREATIVE PERSON!"

Now if you have followed instructions, you should have at least 3 sheets of paper covering P E R S O N A L characteristics pertaining to self, family and business. Each category should consist of at least five separate characteristics, each written out in accordance with the following example:

CAUSE: (characteristic to be achieved)

EFFECT: (a brief statement covering the results to be achieved)

AFFIRMATION: (a brief, positive statement defining the characteristic)

As stated before, taking the time to put these statements down in writing serves a very important purpose: not only does it have the effect of removing your desires from the haphazard realm, it places them in their proper perspective insofar as your Conscious is concerned. Once laid-out in front of you, they become more definitive and specific ...something you must always strive for when dealing with your brain system. I would venture to say the reason that most people fail to achieve, is not so much in the lack of desire as it is in the vagueness in which they address their desires to their memory. Little is ever achieved when expressed in generalities. You should never assume your Conscious knows what you mean. Be specific! Make positive statements! Spell it out in detail! Leave no doubt as to what you wish to accomplish in your plan! And don't throw those sheets of paper away. Save them so you can refer to them occasionally in order to remind your Conscious that you are dead serious about your program.

Okay. What have we accomplished so far? On paper we have listed a number of characteristics, that if followed explicitly, is a sure guarantee for anyone to become successful in any endeavor. Anyone who practices these characteristics can write his or her own ticket to success, because they are "ideally" what any stranger, prospective spouse, employer hopes to find in a person. Aside from these ideal characteristics all that is needed, then, is the potential and capability to carry them out (and you already have that), so all that's left is to displace the restrictive data in your memory that is presently preventing you from becoming such a person.

Okay, as promised, you are now on the threshold of realizing the full implications of the so-far unanswered question: What can I do to change things in my life as I want them to be?

Let's get started.

DATA REVISION

What you are about to become, you are about to make happen.

As stated many times before, your memory cannot tell the difference between an actual experience and one imagined. By means of *mental imagery,* then, you are going to program (input) data into your memory expressing experiences which best portray the concepts of your affirmations ...you're going to literally bombard your memory with verbalized and emotionalized mental pictures of how you want things to be! Before you know it, the experiences of these mental happenings is going to become so prominent in memory that your Conscious will have no other course than to bring them about accordingly. And once underway, your consciously *perceived* experience of it actually happening is going to add still more prominence to the data that's already there. Okay?

At the outset, it is not absolutely necessary, but it would help to speed up the process if you have the proper mental attitude. Although the programming, itself, will bring about the change no matter how negative your attitude may be, it will help to start-up your programming believing each time you impress your mind with an imagined experience, that like dropping a pebble, a rock, or a boulder into a bucket of water, it is causing a definitive effect; that it's just a matter of time before the programmed data will overcome, over-shadow, displace, negate existing data in memory that is contrary to what you are programming into memory; that what you are affirming is, in fact, already an actuality ...the same sense of actuality you have when you plant a seed in the ground, in that you know with assurance it will blossom forth as a like of its kind. As the Bible states: When you pray for something (essentially the same thing as programming), believe you already have it and it will be given unto you accordingly. So give yourself a break. The emotional aspect of already believing will have a greater impact upon your memory than not. Be expectant! Believe in what you are affirming! The more repetition, detail and emotional involvement, the sooner it will become, in fact, a reality. As Reverend Ike said: "You'll get to where you're going much faster if you look like you have already been there." With such an attitude of expectancy, then, let's get on with the programming.

REPROGRAMMING

For reason to be discussed in a later chapter, there are two periods of time when your mind is more receptive to programming than at any other time during your wakeful state: one occurs upon awakening in the morning, and the other occurs prior to going to sleep at night. Being that this altered state of awareness (called Alpha) is a natural daily happening, it would be foolish not to make the most of it.

Once you have committed your affirmations to memory, you should do the following: While in bed, and in a state of total relaxation (preferably) with eyes closed, gently try to picture yourself in the midst of the kind of surroundings you want to be a part of your life while at the same time mentally expressing the words: **"Day by day, in every way, everything in my life is getting better and better!"** Now, instead of seeing yourself in the surroundings (externalizing), try to become that "you" you mentally picture in the surroundings, and begin acting out the roles as defined by your affirmations. Starting out, for instance, you should have the *feeling* of being around people smiling pleasantly while mentally expressing the affirmation, **"I always wear a smile!"** Include as much detail and emotional involvement as possible. Mentally feel yourself playing all the roles you have written out. While mingling with people, feel yourself: *showing a sincere interest in them, encouraging them to talk* *about themselves, calling them by name, being enthusiastic* about it, and above all, *avoiding any sort of argument.* As you feel yourself going through your list of affirmations, mentally express them as written out. The possibilities of the kind of different surroundings you can come up with is unlimited. Just let your imagination go. Above all, while acting-out your roles make sure you also include the kind of feedback (effect) you would expect as a result of what you are affirming. More importantly, keep in mind this is your show; you can make things turn out any way you wish! Also keep in mind that your memory, like a camcorder recording both picture and sound, is recording everything you are projecting upon your mental screen as an actual happening. Be specific and explicit. How you mentally picture yourself and the kind of situations you want to become a part of your life is how the data will show up in your memory. The more repetition, detail and emotional involvement, the greater the impact it will have upon your memory

Now, after all affirmations have been completed, take a moment to reflect upon how great it feels to be the person who possesses all the qualities you have affirmed. Then bring your programming to a close with the statement: **"And so it is!"** All in all it should take you about fifteen or twenty minutes to complete your program.

If you make a practice to program your memory at least twice a day ...morning and night... within several weeks you should begin to notice concrete results taking place in your thoughts, actions and behavior. As these constructive changes begin taking place, the experience of it impressed upon your memory will tend to accelerate the process, in that instead of your memory receiving positive impressions solely from your mental images, it will be complimented and reinforced from your "actual" experiences as well. Before you know it, what you have been affirming will begin to become as natural to you as your present mode of thinking and behavior.

A word of caution, however, don't become complacent. Like all uphill battles, so it is with programming your memory; you must constantly reinforce your progress. Left on its own, like anything else, your brain system will tend to take the path of least resistance, especially if you allow yourself to be subjected to all the depressive and destructive crap put out by the mass-media these days. Remember, you have a lifetime of negative data to over-come, and although it may seem like you have it licked, you still need to reinforce your memory with constructive data in order to keep your Conscious on track.

In referring to your written affirmations, you probably noticed that each of the characteristics has, or can be, readily defined in one word ..."smile," "names," "enthusiastic," etc. In order to help reinforce the programming you are doing in the morning and night, it is suggested you take a 3 X 5 card and list all of the characteristics on it using a single word to cover each. Keep the card in your purse or pocket (as a reminder to use it), and refer to it during the day. There are times between appointments, when you're on a break, moments of inactivity, or just driving around in the car when you can glance at your list and mull the words over. As before, try to mentally picture and feel yourself actively portraying the significance of the affirmations. Consciously attempt to portray yourself in such roles all during your wakeful hours. This kind of practice helps immeasurably in reinforcing what you're attempting to make happen.

Although I have saved this for last, it certainly shouldn't be construed as an after-thought. It, more than all the others, is the most important affirmation you can possibly make. It is that of "MAINTAINING A POSITIVE ATTITUDE AT ALL TIMES!"

A pessimistic attitude is like an acid that constantly eats away at the foundations of what you are trying to construct.

A pessimistic thought should be avoided like the plague. It should be dealt with in the same manner you would treat a poisonous snake; either kill it or give it a wide birth!

Maintaining a positive attitude at all times is probably the most important asset you can ever hope to have. It is the basis upon which the whole idea of self-improvement is based. It is your only defense against failure and fear. It is, believe me, the most important affirmation you can make.

Business for most of us is the source of our bread and butter; it demands a great deal of our time and thought. As a result of becoming actively engaged in business affairs, anyone can suffer a number of disappointments. This can only be overcome by *maintaining a positive attitude at all times*. Without such an attitude to carry you from one disappointment to another, you could be dashed on the rocks of despair, taxing even the most stubborn of us to pick him/herself up and try to get things going again. With a positive mental attitude one doesn't have to consciously pick themselves up when things go wrong; they're already up, they're already confidently prepared to move on to the next crisis.

To insure yourself of not folding under pressure ...a pressure you are bound to encounter as you move-up the ranks from what you are now to what you plan to become tomorrow... it is suggested you make a practice of repeating this affirmation as often as you can throughout the day. Think of it as a protective shield if you like, it will help to negate any and all negative situations you may encounter.

Make a practice of affirming it during your programming sessions, also. Just as the opening beneficial statement ("...getting better and better!") and the closing statement ("And so it is!") serve as blanket instructions to your mind, think of the affirmation, **"I always maintain a positive attitude at all times!"** as the topping on the dessert, the icing on the cake, as the last word. It is the umbrella that covers everything you are trying to do. Repeat it as often as possible. It's surprising what it will do for your confidence.

Now, just a passing word on programming. As you will soon discover, it is by no means a "walk-in-the-park." Nor can you expect it to be. It requires a great deal of mental stamina, primarily because your brain system doesn't like to be shoved around; it fights you at every opportunity because you are trying to upset a pattern that has been established since birth. Your system resists your efforts to take-over just as you would if some stranger came into your domain and told you to "move over buddy, I'm taking charge of things!" If you are persistent with your system you will win the battle, but not without a fight. Over-coming your system's resistance is much like learning to walk for the first time; at first it seems like you're not making headway at all, but after you've learned to take the first step successfully, each successive step becomes that much easier.

In the beginning, as you get your programming sessions under way, you will become aware of your system's resistance to what you are trying to plant in its memory. Pay no attention to it! Your conscious is only reacting to the false data (?) ...according to the present data of record in memory that is, as it naturally would. Keep in mind, however, that each time you impress your memory with an affirmative statement or mental picture, it is definitely making an impression on your memory and subsequently dilutes the prominence of that data which opposes it. The degree of the dilution, of course, will depend upon how much detail and emotion is associated with it. So make a practice of programming often, and include a lot of detail and emotion!

You're probably wondering how long it takes to get results and for how long you should continue your programming. As for results, that, of course, depends upon you and how persistent you are in carrying-out your programming. I would say, however, in most cases, you shouldn't expect all of your programmed characteristics to become effective at the same time; it all depends upon the amount of negative data that needs to be over-come. Some characteristics might become effective within a week. For others, it might take several months. You're going to have to be the judge as to your performance. Once you find yourself comfortably expressing the characteristics you are affirming, you can substitute others to take their place, such as losing weight, curtailing excessive drinking, smoking, improving your golf swing or tennis stroke. Just make sure you employ a plan for each substitute. It's important to give it the mental attention of being definitive and seeing it written-out accordingly.

Once you find you have improved along these lines, substitute with still others. Again, you must be the judge in all such matters. Only you can do the programming, and it is only you whom you are trying to satisfy.

Programming is something successful people purposely or inadvertently practice throughout their life-time: constantly trying to improve themselves and to achieve bigger and better goals. Successful people are successful because they never allow themselves to become stagnant. Each time they reach one plateau they move on to a higher one. See that you do the same.

IT'S UP TO YOU!

Now before we bring this part to a close, let's take just a moment to review the salient points so far discussed. First off, let's make something very clear: If you follow your plan of self-improvement, I promise that you will soon possess the necessary characteristics and qualities to become successful in just about anything you choose to do. The reason I can make such a statement is really quite simple. Anyone who displays the capacity to deal effectively with people (to give them what they want the most ...favorable recognition and appreciation), who is well-groomed, well-mannered, practices good personal hygiene and possesses the capacity to be aggressive, confident, persistent, reliable and creative in everything he or she does are instant winners, both in the eyes of others as well as themselves. And as far as I know, I have never known a winner of any endeavor who was ever considered not successful. It must be remembered, of course, the promise is made on the basis that you possess the qualities mentioned. And should you doubt that such qualities are unavailable to you, in particular, consider the following:

Insofar as the capability and potential to possess such qualities and characteristics is concerned, unless you are suffering from some mental vestige, the fact (as brought-out by the Milwaukee Project) that children born to mothers of IQs of 70 or less (after exposure to acceptable mental stimulation) when tested, showed a general trend of higher IQs than the norm for their age peers; some even registering IQs as high as 135, is indicative that each of us has the necessary mental capabilities to program and retain any sort of data we wish to impress upon our system.

As for the probability your memory will accept and respond to suggestion, your thoughts, in particular ...purposeful or otherwise, the fact that you learn from what you experience is all the proof you need that your memory readily responds to suggestion ...much as it is doing here to the printed words on this page. There is, of course, other proof; hypnosis, for example, all is self hypnosis. And as for whether or not your memory will accept and respond to thought, that should be the most obvious of all. Remember the example of meeting the imagined bear along the trail? walking the plank when raised several stories above the ground? the prominent memory recall of being bitten by a dog because of the emotion associated with it?

What more proof do you need? You have the same degree of potential and capability to achieve as anyone else; you have a brain system that by Nature must accept, retain and respond to any and all suggestion impressed upon it, and now you have a plan designed to cause your system to make you a very desirable person. You have in your possession at this very moment all you need in order to do or become anything you desire! And because you have it, you, alone, are solely responsible for what you do with it. You now have the final answer to the three most important questions you could ever ask of yourself; you now know *what* you must do in order to make things happen in your life as you want them to be! Yes, you now have all the keys to the proverbial candy store. Now, make the most of it!

THE REAL CAUSE

Before we move on, this is as good a time as any to take a few minutes to apply what's been covered so far. At this point in time you should have a better-than-before understanding of both yourself and others. And knowing that *each of us is what we are because of what we have experienced in the past,* you should have a better understanding of *why* our society is suffering from the myriad of ills it is today. It should be obvious to you, for instance, that as long as brain systems, especially those of the young, are indiscriminately and blatantly exposed to acts of sexual promiscuity, violence, crime, abuse, etc., more than often portrayed under the guise of "entertainment" by the various media, that they will be mirrored and further perpetuated throughout our society. Such was not the belief of our U. S. Surgeon General, Luther Terry, back in the early 60's, however. He said: "...it's absolutely not true that television has an influencing affect upon the public." The same message was parroted by the motion picture industry, the "girly" magazines and all those who profit from the proliferation of such junk.

To those who honestly believe such lies, I say, convince me it isn't so. Convince me, for example, that there is no direct correlation between the "first" successful high jacking of an airplane reported on TV (which subsequently inspired TV dramas and theatrical productions that appeared shortly in the media thereafter) and the sudden popular high jacking incidents of planes that were and still are occurring all over the world. Convince me that the first student riot (reported nationally) which took place at the University of California at Berkeley, didn't inspire the raft of student rioting all over the nation which followed shortly thereafter. Convince me that what little use of marijuana taking place in the nation in the 50s has not been escalated into a popular issue today because of indiscriminate legislation and over-reporting by the mass media. Convince me, also, that the youths who, by their own admission, poured gasoline over a victim and set her on fire were not inspired by the same act portrayed on a TV program shown the night before. Hey, we're talking about what took place in the 50s and 60s. And after spending trillions of tax-payer money trying to curtail such acts, our government hasn't yet made a dent in stopping it. The media is totally out of control. And yet the powers that be are still trying to tell us that the mass media has no influencing affect upon the public. If you buy into that hogwash, just consider the billions of dollars spent on advertising every year ...TV, newspapers, magazines, radio, billboards, the tobacco industry, do you honestly believe that people are not influenced by what the advertising industry and the mass media are subjecting us to? Get real! Knowing what you now know about your brain system and how it operates, it should be obvious to you that whatever happenings one experiences, good or bad, that they are faithfully recorded and become a part of the memory. And whether they be portrayed in the form of entertainment, educational, advertising, or whatever, repeated exposure to any form of experience ...especially decadent acts due to the emotion involved on the part of the viewer, it's going to have an adverse affect upon those who experience it. It's the same old story of the pebbles dropped into a bucket of water: each experience, good or bad, makes its mark on the memory, and

unless one purposely makes a conscious effort to discredit the
negative experiences at the outset, any repetition of same is
eventually going to over-come all opposition to it in the
memory system. Repeated enough times without
accompanying opposition, it will eventually become acceptable
and in turn affect one's thoughts and behavior accordingly
(just as I hope the positive data revision you will be doing will
shortly become acceptable and in turn affect your thoughts
and behavior accordingly).

Just as it is happening to you right now and every single
moment of your wakeful life, your system is being incessantly
impressed with a variety of impressions (experiences)
stemming from your surroundings. Some are beneficial.
Some are not. All experiences are influential in one form or
another, and without realizing it, it is possible for your
concepts to be altered without your knowing it. How else, for
instance, is it possible for someone to voluntarily want to end
their life (suicide) unless the repeated exposure to adverse
information is unknowingly unopposed and allowed to over-
come all opposition to it in the system? How else can you
account for the inhuman acts which took place in the
concentration camps of WW II and Boznia and Kosavo in the
'90s unless the people who carried them out were not
influenced in the absence of any conscious opposition to it?
The same holds true of anyone who is subjected to repeated
exposure to the use of drugs, committing violent acts,
breaking the law, etc., it becomes an accepted concept in the
memory of those who make no conscious effort to discredit it
...so it will be in their life accordingly. It can be no other way.

With or without your help, your goal-seeking learning-
machine brain system is going to function the only way eons
of evolutionary time have programmed it to do: its actions are
going to be influenced the "greatest" by whatever it
experiences the "mostest." And in spite of the fact that your
memory may presently contain virtuous concepts in every
respect, that alone is no guarantee that they will remain so

without reinforcement, because nothing is permanent in the memory ...permanent in the sense that once a concept is formed that it will remain forever. For if such were true, it would be the equivalent of assuming that once you formed an opinion of something, you could never change it, which we know from our own experiences is not the case.

Perhaps you are wondering why I have brought all this up. Admittedly, I am shocked and more than disturbed with the ignorance and incompetence which prevails today at all levels of federal, state and local government, in public education and politics. But more importantly, it's imperative that you become aware of what is happening in your surroundings and why; to understand that much of what you are exposed to daily is not what could be truly considered in your best interest, and that if you don't oppose it when you find the slightest hint of questionable ability, it's quite possible for the adverse aspects of your surroundings to quietly establish a foothold in your memory system while displacing otherwise virtuous concepts and causing you to possibly think and act in terms of how someone or some faction might be wanting you to do. In other words, I'm suggesting that you do not allow yourself to be gradually influenced by the general decay of morals, principles and virtues that are becoming more and more prevalent in our surroundings today. Beware of anything and everything in your surroundings which does not truly express your best interests. Don't allow yourself, for instance, to be influenced into thinking that the rising crime rate is going to be solved by increasing the ranks of law enforcement and the confiscation of all citizens hand guns, because it isn't. Such alternatives may seem harmless enough in the name of protecting the public, but they are not. The more regulation you allow to be placed upon you and your surroundings, the more your individual rights are being usurped right out from under you ...not what I would consider to be in yours or my best interest.

When an act of crime, violence, or anything else of that nature is committed, it is not because there is a shortage of law enforcement personnel or a surplus of hand guns available, it's because those who commit such acts do so out of frustration; a frustration brought about by their inability to cope with their surroundings intelligently. And why are they unable to cope with their surroundings intelligently while at the same time others are? You already know the answer: it's because of the nature of the information in their memory systems resulting from what they have experienced from their surroundings. It's that simple, as is the solution to all of our social problems, including the school shooting that took place in Littleton, Colorado in '99.

Those who commit acts of crime and violence are no different from anyone else. They have the same needs and desires as you and I, and they have the same potential and capability as any one else to do or become whatever they want. It's just that they are not aware that they have *it* (potential and capability). And not being aware of *it* is like not knowing *it* at all. If they don't experience *it* early in life from their parents; if they don't experience *it* in school; if they don't experience *it* in their religious institutions, on the theater screen, in printed matter, or on the TV, where, then, are they going to experience *it*?

Contrary to what the general public is led to believe, acts of violence are not curtailed by force or the infringement upon the rights of others; they can only be intelligently dealt with by displacing the causative agent responsible. Change the causative information by overcoming it with constructive information (beginning with an understanding of self) and there will be no further reasoning in the brain system to commit such acts. Again, as Socrates said: ...anyone who truly knows himself will succeed, for he will know precisely wherein his capabilities lie and the area in which to apply them; whereas one who doesn't know himself, he will frequently blunder, even to the point of ruining his life. I know with assurance, that had our crime infested cities, instead of adding more law enforcement officers to fight a rising crime rate 20 years ago, put their efforts into the education of the young in matters of morality, values, credibility, integrity and responsibility, and especially an exposure to the kind of self-insight we've covered so far, anyone today could walk any street in America at night without the fear of being molested. The same logic is true for all social problems and ills.

Knowledge as opposed to regulation, it's as simple as that. All regulation evolves as an attempt to treat an effect. Knowledge, on the other hand, treats the cause directly. Remove the splinter ...the cause, from an inflamed finger, and the infection will go away. Try to treat the infection without removing the splinter and it will persist and only get worse. Hopefully you will keep this in mind the next time you find yourself suffering from some adversity. As always, the cause for everything you think and do lies in the files of your memory system. If it proves to be undesirable, displace it with mental experiences depicting how you want it to be, and the adversity will subside and go away. Dwell upon the adversity, however, and the prominence of it will increase further, exacerbating the condition. As you will find, this is true in every aspect of the human experience.

POTENTIAL

Man's main task in life is to give birth to himself, to become what he potential is.
Dr. Erich Fromm

It's time to talk about another kind of potential besides that of programming our system to do our bidding ...a potential we all have in common, but few of us realize we have it or know how to use it.

Undoubtedly you are familiar with the success stories of Andrew Carnegie, John D. Rockerfeller, Alexander Graham Bell, F.W.Woolworth, King Gillette, Henry Ford, George Eastman, George Washington Carver, to name a few; men who accumulated vast fortunes from humble beginnings. The truth is these men had no more potential than any one of us has at this moment. What set them apart from others was that they didn't accept the precept of not being able to do anything about their lives; they either stumbled upon or sought the source of their potential and learned how to work with it. There are, of course, better things in life than building vast empires and making large amounts of money. But regardless of what they may be, the chances of it becoming manifest in the life of someone who recognizes and learns to work with the source of his or her potential is far greater than for someone who doesn't. With this in mind I would now like to expose you to some cases of so-called psychic phenomena that demonstrate the kind of potential I am referring to:

Thomas Fuller, an African Negro born in 1710 and taken to Virginia as a slave, could do arithmetic mentally, including such feats as multiplying two nine-digit numbers together. Yet he never learned to read or write.

A six-year old child in Vermont was found able to factorize any number up to a million in his head. Given 171,395 he knew instantly it was the product of 5, 7, 59 and 83. For 247,483 he correctly stated 941 and 263. Asked how he was able to perform such feats in his head, he replied: "God tells me."

Wolfgang Mozart, who produced over 600 works before his death at age 35, learned to play the harpsichord at the age of 4. He started composing music at age 5. When he was six he played for the Austrian empress and her court.

Today there are patients in mental institutions who can tell promptly when certain holidays will fall in years picked at random, or the day that some day of the week will be several hundred years from now or in the past. They can add up a dozen numbers as fast as they are called out. They can glance at a typewritten page and tell the exact number of words. But they don't recall the names of the doctors who see them daily.

Charles Lindbergh's story as related in the book "The Spirit of St. Louis" is more than a tale of his historic flight across the Atlantic. It reveals much of the super-human battle he waged in trying to stay wake. Here, in brief, is what he said occurred: He talked about the fuselage being crowded with ghostly human presence. That they seemed able to disappear or show themselves at will. That sometimes their voices spoke out, familiar voices, advising him on his flight, encouraging him to prevail. That it was like a reunion of friends after separation, "as though I've known them before in some past incarnation."

The following appeared in the Hearst papers of April 27 and 28, 1938, being a copyrighted account of an interview with Henry Ford: "When I was a young man I, like so many others, was bewildered. I found myself asking the question, 'what are we here for?' I found no answer. Without some answer to that question life is empty, useless. Then one day a friend handed me a book. That little book gave me the answer I was seeking. It changed my whole life. From emptiness and uselessness, it changed my outlook upon life to purpose and meaning. I believe that we are here now and will come back again ...Of this I am sure... that we are here for a purpose. And that we go on. Mind and memory... they are the eternals."

Another interview with Ford as reported by George Sylvester Viereck of the San Francisco Examiner, August 28, 1928: I adopted the theory of Reincarnation when I was twenty six. ...religion offered nothing to the point... even work could not give me complete satisfaction. Work is futile if we cannot utilize the experience we collect in one life in the next. When I discovered Reincarnation it was as if I had found a universal plan. I realized that there was a chance to work out my ideas. Time was no longer limited. I was no longer a slave to the hands of the clock... Genius is experience. Some think that it is a gift or talent, but it is the fruit of long experience in many lives. Some are older souls than others, and so they know more.

It is common knowledge that in retrogressing patients back in age while undergoing hypnotherapy that they will occasionally mention experiences and display voice, language, handwriting and other colloquial characteristics of a previous lifetime(s) that had taken place, fifty, a hundred, and even several thousand years before. One such famous case was that recorded in a book written by Morey Bernstein's "The Search for Bridey Murphy." In brief, Bridey Murphy is a story of Ruth Simmons, a young housewife living in Pueblo, Colorado. One evening in 1952 she agreed to be the subject of a hypnotic experiment. The hypnotist was a young businessman, Morey Bernstein. At first he led her back through what we commonly call age-regression. Eventually she remembered the toys she loved when she was only one year old. There was nothing unusual about this, but in a second session the hypnotist suggested, "your mind will be going back ...back until you find yourself in some other scene, in some other place, in some other time. You will be able to talk to me about it and answer my questions."

The gist of her response was that she was a little Irish girl named Bridey Murphy, who lived in Cork with her mother Kathleen, her barrister father Duncan, and one brother ...the year was 1806. She told how, at fifteen, she attended Mrs. Strayne's school in Cork "studying to be a lady," and how she later married Brian MacCarthy and went to live in Belfast. As the session continued, all recorded on tape, the life story carried on through the years, up to Bridey's death at age sixty-six. She claimed that, after bodily death, Bridey existed in the spirit world for forty years, then was reborn in Iowa, in 1923, to take up her life as Ruth ...the present Ruth Simmons.

Checking later with the Irish Consulate, the British Information Service, the New York Public Library and other sources, Mr. Bernstein learned that a number of Bridey's statements were consistent with historical fact. Ruth had never visited Ireland.

Asked: "Do you believe a man has a soul?" Thomas Edison's reply was: "No one understands that man is not a unit of life. He is as dead as granite. The unit of life is composed of swarms of billions of highly charged entities which live in cells. I believe that when a man dies, this swarm deserts the body and goes out into space, but keeps on and enters another cycle of life and is immortal." ..."The more we learn the more we realize that there is life in things we used to regard as inanimate, as lifeless."

World-famous author Janet Taylor Caldwell relates in the book "In Search for A Soul" (Jess Stern, Doubleday and Co,) many revealing and startling details of a number of previous lives removed while she was under hypnosis. Despite her own skepticism, this credible and well-thought-of author reveals recollections which proved to be the basis for many of her novels, for they contained material of which she claims no conscious knowledge. The book, "Testimony of Two Men", for instance, could only have been written by someone with authentic medical understanding. Yet Janet has no known knowledge of medicine.

There are, of course, many more accountable writings on the subject of rebirth, reincarnation, life-hereafter, etc., especially in the works of Edna Farber, Ernest Seton (founder of the Boy Scouts), Rudyard Kipling, H. G. Wells, Somerset Maugham, Jack London, Robert Stroud (Birdman of Alcatraz), Pearl S. Buck, Aldous Huxley, Louis Bromfield, Thomas Huxley (Biologist), William James (Psychologist), Luther Burbank, Mahandas Gandhi, Bertrand Russell (Mathematician), Carl S. Jung (Psychologist), Gustof Strombey (Astronomer), Sir Julian Huxley (Biologist), J. B. Rhine (Parapsychologist), Emerson, Benjamin Franklin, Victor Hugo, Plato, Edgar Allen Poe, Tolstoy and Mark Twain, to name a few.

Perhaps you have heard or read of the works of Edgar Cayce, famous American psychic (1877-1945)? If you haven't you should make the effort. Cayce had the ability to accurately diagnose illnesses of people he had never met while in a self-imposed trance (an altered state of mental awareness) even though they were separated by distances of hundreds of miles. With nothing more to go on than a letter received from a subject miles away asking for help, Cayce would call in his stenographer, and usually in the presence of a number of qualified witnesses, put himself into a trance and begin a commentary of his findings while examining the absent body of the patient. More than often his descriptions indicated that he was actually in the subject's body checking this organ and that, all the while his findings were being carefully recorded by his stenographer. Considering that most of Cayce's subjects asked for his help only after exhausting all so-called legitimate medical resources, the cures he effected were something to behold.

The fact that Cayce had no known previous knowledge of medicine was even more remarkable. Often he would prescribe medicines that were never heard of. And when they were unavailable at the local pharmacy, he would describe their contents and have them prepared. In one instance he prescribed a medicine that a pharmacist couldn't fill because of one particular ingredient that could not be located. In hearing of this by correspondence, Cayce put himself into a trance and proceeded to mentally project himself to the location of the particular pharmacy miles away and began searching around the storeroom where the various chemicals were kept. Finding what he was looking for hidden behind a bottle of a seldom-used solution, he sent a letter to the pharmacist as to its location, and was later informed that it was located exactly where he said it was in spite of the fact that he had never physically set foot in the place in his whole life.

Another psychic you may have heard of is Peter Hurkos, the Dutchman house painter who fell from a ladder two stories high and landed on his head and suddenly found he had psychic tendencies. Primarily, he is noted for locating lost people and solving homicides all over the world. It seems that all he has to do is touch something that has been used or worn by the person, and it "turns him on" to the point that he can mentally picture the subject wherever he or she may be at the moment. As for helping to solve homicides, all he has to do is visit the scene of the crime, and more than often he can tell you what took place and describe in detail the people that took part in it. He is known for his premonition also. Often he described happenings in great detail that had not yet taken place, but did so at a later date, just as he described them to be.

Another Dutch psychic, Gerard Crosiet. was consulted by the police in the murder case involving three civil-rights workers in Mississippi, and according to reports he claimed to have received by ESP (extra sensory perception), he was able to give accurate information and descriptions not only of the area where the bodies were buried, but also that local policemen were involved in the killings.

A number of years ago, Dr. Olga Worral, internationally known psychic healer, was invited to participate in a series of experiments conducted at the Agnes Scott College in the state of Georgia. The key experiment had the objective of determining whether or not some type of measurable energy is given off by a "healer's" hands while doing his or her thing. A cloud chamber, a device used by scientists to measure high energy particles, was used as the detector. The experiment involved Dr. Worral placing her hands at the side of the chamber without touching it, much as she does in the "laying-on of hands" with her patients. It was observed that a wave pattern developed in the vacuum chamber, and as she shifted the position of her hands so did the energy wave move accordingly. Later, a follow-up experiment was conducted to see if Dr. Worral could affect the cloud chamber from a distance. At the time when it was determined the chamber had reached a state of stabilization the Dr. was telephoned and asked to concentrate her thoughts and energies upon the chamber in Georgia, some 600 miles away. It was suggested, at a prescribed time, she mentally picture the act of holding her hands at the outside of the imagined chamber for several minutes, then shift their position ninety degrees just as she did during the first experiment. Prior to the phone call, a fine, uniform mist was visible in the chamber. Approximately three minutes after the prescribed time the experiment was to commence, a definite change began to take place. The mist began to pulsate and dark waves began to appear, but they did not change direction. Fifteen minutes later a call was put in to Dr. Worral and she was asked if she had changed the position of her hands as requested earlier. Her reply was that she didn't.

Nelya Mikailova, the psychokineses medium of Russia has stopped the pendulum of wall clocks, moved plastic cases, water pitchers weighing over one pound and assorted dishes, cups and glasses, among other things. PK, as it is called, is an ability to move matter while at a distance without physically touching it.

Besides commanding such things as bread, matches, cigarettes, apples, etc. to jump off a table, she has been known to separate the white from the yoke of a raw egg, placed in a saline solution, from six feet away.

Karl Niklolaiev, another Russian psychic, contacted his friend miles away using mental telepathy. Both were supervised by scientific teams, and at a prearranged time, Uri Kamensky was handed a sealed package selected at random from a number of similar boxes. Upon opening it he began to finger the object contained within it. The object was a metal spring of seven tight spirals. Within minutes, Karl Niolaiev, some 1800 miles away, wrote down his impression of what his friend Yuri was trying to transmit. He wrote: "round, metallic ...gleaming ...indented ...looks like a coil."

Under doubly strict laboratory conditions at Stanford University, Uri Geller beat one-trillion to one odds by guessing 12 out of 12 times in different experiments which 10 double sealed cans held a steel ball and 15 cans held water.

By correctly calling the face-up numbers on a die (singular of dice) in a sealed box eight out of eight times, Geller beat one-million to one odds. He was also able to create a magnetic field " ...presumably through psychic energy" and affect the weight, both plus and minus, of a one-gram object.

In yet another experiment, Geller was placed in a room shielded visually, acoustically and electrically from drawings he was asked to duplicate. He did so ten out of ten times.

Pat Price, a former Police Commissioner of Burbank, California, was noted for his remote viewing ...the ability to describe randomly selected unfamiliar sites up to a thousand miles away. An article in Nature Magazine observed: "Price's ability to describe correctly, buildings, docks, roads, gardens, building construction material, color ambiance and activity sometimes in great detail, indicated the functioning of remote perceptual ability." By the way, much of these experiments were documented and shown on PBS some years back. The program was "NOVA" and the title of the program was E.S.P.

During World War II countless cases were reported of mothers and sweethearts on the home-front who sensed the exact moment their sons or loved ones were killed or injured on some battlefield far away.

An experienced angler takes his five-year old son out fishing in a boat, baits his hook, drops the line in the water and says, "Okay son, when you feel a tug on the line, pull up on the rod like this." In the meantime the father baits his own hook and drops it right next to his son's. Would you care to guess who catches the first fish? The most fish? But of course, the five-year old. This is by no means a rarity. It happens all the time. It is a well-known experience of so-called "beginners' luck."

Have you ever seen anyone walking back and forth across some barren ground with a forked stick held out in front of him, when it suddenly takes a dip down-ward as though there was a fighting ten-pound trout on the other end? That's right, such people are known as diviners, dowsers, or whatever you want to call them. Are they successful in finding what they're looking for? You bet. People looking for water, oil, gas, gold, or whatever, are willing to invest thousands of dollars on just the fact that the diviner's rod indicates the presence of what they're looking for. People don't spend that kind of money just to be entertained.

To locate lifeless matter often 100 feet or more below the surface with nothing more than a forked stick to point the way defies all that is continuum, and yet it is successfully taking place every day. Teams of diviners have been known to locate seams of lead only three inches thick at depths of 500 feet.

Back in 1976 a 12-year old boy lifted the front end of a 3,400 pound automobile so his father, trapped beneath when a jack broke, could roll free.

Rosa Kuleshona can read fine newsprint with her elbow. She can also differentiate color with her finger tips.

In August of 1983 an Ohio fisherman was struck by lightning while taking shelter from a storm. He claims he thought he was dead. Because his heart had stopped, nearby campers administered cardiopulmonary resuscitation until paramedics arrived. After his recovery the victim stated: "I know this sounds weird, but I could see myself in the ambulance and them giving me electric shocks to start my heart. The funny part was that at the time I was dead, I didn't mind; I was floating around having a good time.

The young salmon spends years at sea then comes back to its own river, and what's more, travels up the side of the river which flows the tributary in which it was born. What brings it back definitely? If a salmon going up a river is transferred to another tributary it will at once realize it is in the wrong place and will fight its way down to the main stream and turn up against the current to finish its destiny.

Have you heard the story of the eels? These amazing creatures migrate from all over the world and wind-up in the abysmal deeps south of Bermuda. There they breed and die. The little ones, with no apparent means of knowing anything, start back and find their way to the shores from which their parents came, only to return to Bermuda waters after they have grown to maturity to complete the cycle. Interestingly enough, no American eel has ever been caught in European waters, and no European eel has ever been caught in American waters. Another interesting point, Nature, or whatever, has delayed the maturity of the European eel to compensate for its longer journey as compared to the American eel.

Ascension Island is so far from anywhere that even a good navigator has trouble finding it at times. Yet sea turtles from Brazilian waters navigate through 1400 miles of turbulent seas, strong currents and changing tides to hit a stretch of sandy beach with pin point accuracy.

The incredible Blackpole warbler from New England, weighing less than a fifty-cent piece, makes an annual non-stop, over-water flight of more than 2300 miles to South America only to return to the tree and branch from which it started.

Remove a Honey bee from each of three separate hives placed next to each other. Identify each bee with a different colored mark on its back and set out a dish of sugar and water a long distance away. Then release the three bees and they will locate the nectar. Once located, each bee will return to its respective hive and relate its findings to its fellow bees as to the source, distance and direction, whereupon they will load-up with just enough nectar from the hive to make the outgoing trip and return fully loaded with the new nectar.

Today it is common to hear of people communicating with their plants. Is it by coincidence that those who claim to love their plants also produce healthy, fruitful specimens?

Back in early February, 1966, Cleve Baxter, formally with the C.I.A., who operates a training school for law enforcement officers in the techniques of the polygraph (lie detector), was fooling around with a philodendron plant wondering if he could measure the rate at which water rose from its root structure into its leaves. Being hooked-up to the polygraph, the plant was putting out a normal tracing as the paper moved under the sensitive stylus. By shear accident, Baxter gave serious thought to burning one of the plant's leaves in order to stimulate it, and at that instant the stylus went wild, scribing dramatic waves across the paper under it. Aware that he had not moved, touched the plant or machine, Baxter's curiosity was greatly aroused. He decided to explore further to see if what he dared to believe was really true; that the plant actually sensed his thoughts. Purchasing some live brine shrimp and dropping them into boiling water out of view of the plant, he could see, even from where he was, that at the moment the shrimp were dropped in the water the stylus leaped frantically across the paper removing any doubts that plants do sense the emotions of other living things.

In more recent experiments Baxter has found that fresh fruit, vegetables, yeast, blood, paramecium, and even scrapings from the roof of a person's mouth all show a sensitivity to other life forms in distress. Not only has a response been clearly measured between things of the same kind (when one is tested the other reacts) but between very dissimilar subjects as well: Baxter attached the electrodes of his machine to a plant down the hall while he broke an egg to be eaten in the lab kitchen. The plant strenuously objected. Then he tested one egg while breaking a second egg. The response was equally violent ...an example of similar and dissimilar subjects.

Recently, Baxter was so elated with the success of his experiments, he claimed ...and has since proven... that plants can be used in solving homicides. To prove his point he had two men from the local police department flip a coin to see who was going to step into his laboratory and "kill" one of two plants. When it was decided who the "murderer" was to be, he, the bad guy, walked into the lab and cut one of the plants to ribbons and walked out. Some time later, Baxter rounded-up a number of off-duty volunteers to assist him in completing the experiment. Once he hooked-up his machine to the remaining plant (the "witness" to the "crime") Baxter had each of the volunteers ...including the bad guy (known

only to Baxter). march by the remaining plant one at a time
while an official of the department watched the reaction of
the plant being monitored. To the official's utter dismay, the
stylus suddenly went bananas the moment one of the
"suspects" entered the room. And as you may well guess, it
was indeed the man who had committed the "crime."

As a child I recall reading many exciting books about
animals ...dogs, cats, horses, burros, bears, and the like...
that more than often befriended man in a variety of ways.
In particular were the reports of dogs and cats traveling
hundreds of miles across unfamiliar terrain to join their
master who had either left them on purpose, or lost them at
some other location. As it was explained to me at the time: it
was possible because animals have a keen sense of smell. I
didn't buy that explanation at the time, nor do I buy it now
...especially now. Anyone in their right mind should be
astute enough to know that no sense of smell could pick-up
an owner's scent that had covered long distances inside a
car riding on tires over well-traveled highways.

Personally, I've never experienced such happenings, but
I do, and have had animals around most of my life, and I
know that without a spoken word or change in expression,
most of them have been able to read my thoughts like a book,
and I theirs.

Chances are you've come across the belief that animals
can tell when people fear them because of some sort of tell-
tale odor that is given-off. The same is believed to be true
about insects; the bee, for instance, who, if sensing your fear
when it lands on you will plant its stinger. I've often
wondered: if such a supposition is true, is there also an odor
we emit when we don't fear, but instead admire and
appreciate an animal or insect? Such is ridiculous! I can
certainly appreciate that people "put-out" something
animals and insects can sense. But it's certainly not odors.
I choose to believe it's thought; thought that is transmitted
and received over some common incorporeal common

frequency or channel; a common channel which ties all of creation together.

Perhaps you have read about some of the experiments that were carried-out some years ago in Russia. One in particular that caught my attention involved newly born ducklings that were removed from their mother shortly after birth and transported by a submarine hundreds of miles away. While submerged, and at a prescribed time, each of the ducklings was killed one at a time while at the same time the reactions of the mother were being recorded on an electroencephalograph (EEG) machine. Clear evidence that the mother sensed each separate demise at the precise moment it occurred was indicated!

Just for the record, I have personally witnessed much of the phenomena described. And there's much more I haven't even mentioned. I have, for instance, witnessed a Garu in Singapore control the flame of a candle. I have seen so-called minstrels walk on sand without leaving foot prints. I have seen and photographed (16mm color) children in India pass the equivalent of a shish kabob skewer through their bodies, showing no sign of pain or blood. I have done the same with fanatics slashing the flesh of their backs to the bone with bolo knives, and again, show no sign of pain or bleeding. I have recorded the complete fire walking ceremony in Fiji on film where men walk on white-hot rocks and show no evidence of burned flesh on their feet when they're through. As a youngster I saw Grace Wiley soothe (with talk) a vicious, provoked rattle snake into uncoiling and stretching itself full length on a table in front of an audience at her "Zoo for Happiness" near Long Beach, California. Not only did the six-foot rattler stretch out full length, it rested its head inches from where she was standing while she proceeded to stroke its back and it responding by arching its back in cat-like fashion.

Now before you dismiss all of this as fantasy, trickery or so much hog-wash, let me again remind you why you might feel this way. In assessing any experience impressed upon your memory, your Conscious is compelled to evaluate it on the basis of what *you have* experienced in the past. For most of us, the nature of such phenomena is beyond our comprehension; we have no logical explanation for it according to the data of record in our memories. Therefore, the tendency is to discount it as being somebody's pipe dream and let it go at that. This is understandable; no one wants to be made out as a fool; it's not the kind of favorable recognition we are seeking. So to those of you who find it difficult to accept the fact that people, such as Cayce, are able to do what they do, I strongly suggest you drop by Virginia Beach, Virginia and visit the Cayce Institute, as I did. Everything Cayce did (and I only touched upon a few of his 1,400 "readings") is well documented and attested to by many prominent men and women. Or better yet, try to attend a symposium on Parapsychology that might be held at one of the large universities near you. Talk to the people involved. Most of them are MDs, PHDs, or have a number of degrees in the field of science. Listen to what they have to say. They can tell you about things that will blow your mind.

Speaking of blowing one's mind, Have you ever seen or heard of Kirlian photography? Well let me tell you about it: Today, science has come to see all material things, including bone, flesh and tissue of the human body as not being solid, but rather as a collection of the substance which accounts for matter and energy, i.e., a collection of atoms. In short, when a particular manifestation of atoms combine into a variety of visible forms, we are seeing these visible forms of atoms as matter. And when a particular manifestation of atoms combine into a variety of invisible forms, although they are not seen, they do in fact exist ...as depicted by scientific instruments... but as atoms in forms of energy.

We are all familiar with matter, of course. But what about the other side of the coin? Is there evidence that such forms of energy do, in fact, exist? You be the judge: Kirlian photography is photography that utilizes high frequency electrical fields to produce an image on sensitized film. Essentially, the object to be photographed, be it metal, leather, plastic, parts of the human anatomy, flowers, leaves, or whatever is placed over a piece of film or paper which is inserted between two metal plates wired to a generator. When turned on the generator produces a high frequency field between the plates which in turn cause the object to radiate some sort of bio-luminescent image onto the film or paper.

My first experience with Kirlian photography was back in 1973 while attending a parapsychology symposium held at the University of California at Los Angeles (UCLA). Dr. Thelma Moss, who at the time headed the department, showed us colored slides of some of the experiments she and her staff had done. Of particular interest were the slides of human hands, and leaves taken from a common household plant.

As for the images produced, the pictures of a hand placed flat on the metal plates, for instance, showed an aura or corona of blue, white, red and green light, possibly one-eighth to one-quarter of an inch protruding from the outline of the hand. At the finger tips, including the thumb, the aura pattern was different. Instead of a seemingly uniform over-spraying of light silhouetting the shape of hand and fingers, it looked as though the tips of the fingers and thumb were generating pointed shapes of light extending in some cases several inches beyond the tips. Again, the emitted light was multi-colored.

Of particular interest was an experiment involving a "faith-healer" and the "laying-on of hands." Prior to the laying-on of hands, both the faith healer's hands and those of the patient were photographed. Both healer and patient had an aura around their hands. There was a contrast difference, however. The healer's hands showed a bright and vibrant aura with long and pointed shapes of light extending from the fingers as opposed to the patients weak and almost faint aura.

Moments after the laying-on of hands was completed, both healer and patient's hands were re-photographed. The results distinctively showed that whatever energy or power was present in the healer's hands had been transferred to the patient!

The aura of light, which has come to be regarded by many as evidence of a possible "life-force," was also present in the case of photographing a geranium leaf. The shape of the aura was unlike that outlining the hand, however. It was, instead, jagged, like the teeth of a saw blade or the flames seen coming from the burner on a gas stove. In any event, hand or leaf, the aura outline in each case was brilliant and multi-colored, which brings us to the point of all this: Dr. Moss did a most unique experiment with a leaf.

Having Kirlian photographed a geranium leaf in its entirety, she proceeded to cut-off a sizable portion of its tip and re-photographed the leaf as before. The result was astounding. Even though one-third of the leaf had been removed, the aura image was the same as if the leaf were whole and intact! Dr. Moss followed this same line of experimenting by taking other leaves, photographing them whole as well as with parts removed. In each case, whether outer extremities or inner areas were removed, the patterns of light and aura remained the same as if the leaf were whole. The question this brings to mind is, could this be an indication of the "flip-side" of matter, an energy impression or form of the whole leaf that does not change even though its counter-part (matter) has been altered? Possibly it is. However, as said before, it was an experiment, and there is still much to be learned before it can be considered conclusive. Nevertheless, it cannot be dismissed that "something" did remain even though the matter side of the leaf had been removed. Was it the energy equivalent of the matter side of the leaf? Perhaps the answer can be found in what's to follow.

Okay, even though I've barely touched upon the subject, from the extent of the evidence presented so far it should be quite obvious that we are involved with something extraordinary that dramatically demonstrates the kind of potential I am certain is innate within each of us. Claims of having lived other lives? Locating lifeless matter hundreds of feet underground with the aid of a stick? Separating the white of an egg from its yoke from six feet away without touching it? Describing happenings in great detail that had not yet taken place? Healing by the "laying-on of hands?" Probing a person's body, effecting cures, locating objects in strange places while hundreds of miles away? Transferring and receiving thought patterns from great distances? Creatures navigating over thousands of miles of ocean with pin-point accuracy? Plants responding to human emotions? What's it all about?

When dealing with matters such as this, who's to really say with authority what is true and what isn't? I don't believe anyone can, because there is no scientific basis at this point in time for dealing with such phenomena. And besides, like the problem of giving a scientific explanation of good and evil, beauty and ugliness, order and freedom, life and death, God, I don't think the kind of phenomena we've covered is yet open to the analytical methods of science. But a philosophical synthesized interpretation? Perhaps. After all, science gives us knowledge, but only philosophy can give us wisdom.

What the evidence seems to tells us is that in order for this so-called phenomena to do what it does requires that it be carried out in some sort of common *medium* that provides a means for the exchange of *communication* between plants, animals and man, i.e. Cleve Baxter's experiments, beginner's luck, telepathy, dowsing, etc.; a medium that also serves as a *source of knowledge* that can be tapped, i.e. Edison's inventions, Mozart's early compositions, intuition, reincarnation, etc.; a medium that provides a means for *incorporeal travel and perception*, i.e., Edgar Cayce, Pat Price, Hurkos, etc.; and a medium that operates on the basis of *energy or life-force* (?) that can be exerted or utilized, i.e., Dr. Olga Worral, Nelya Mikailova, etc. Assuming this to be a possibility, how do we make sense of it? I'm going to attempt to tell you. And please bear with me. I believe it will all make sense in the end.

A MATTER OF PRINCIPLE

It is said, we have our being in a universe of harmony and orderliness. Does this mean the state of the universe is wonderful, good, beautiful, pleasant? No. Harmony and orderliness has nothing to do with such things. It's just another way of saying that everything in the universe is consistent and in accordance: that the sun always rises and sets, that the rivers always run down hill, that the stars and planets are always in their respective positions in the night sky, that your car always starts in the morning (provided all its parts are in harmony), that a fatal gun shot to the head always produces death, that abusing certain drugs can become addictive, that adding sugar to your coffee always gives it a sweeter taste, that when zinc and sulfuric acid are combined hydrogen gas is always produced. The point is, we reside in a universe of consistency and accord.

What's responsible for the accord and consistency is attributed mainly to the influence of so-called natural laws, i.e., the law of gravity, the law of thermodynamics, the law of nature, the laws of force and motion, etc., in that they uniformly influence events in galactic space in the same manner as they do here on planet earth. That's why, with our understanding of the nature of these laws and working in accordance with them, that we are able to send a probe billions of miles out into space with pin point accuracy to explore parts of our solar system and have it successfully return its findings. In short, what gives us the sense that we reside in a universe of harmony and orderliness is that the universe, as we know it, operates in conjunction with natural laws; the same laws responsible for the phenomena just discussed to take place.

So, other than the fact that natural law is behind the harmony and orderliness of the universe, how do we equate natural law to the possible existence of such things as a *medium* common to all things, a *source* of knowledge, *incorporeal* travel and perception, and energy or life force? I believe this can be answered by understanding what it is that gives any law the means to influence outcomes as natural law seems to do.

Because the term Natural Law is familiar with the majority of us, I have used it here to explain the state of the universe. Now, and it shouldn't make any difference to you, I would like to substitute Natural Law with that of Principle since, in essence, both are generally regarded essentially the same; it's just a matter of how they're interpreted. I'll explain:

Principle can be defined: *as the ultimate source, origin, or cause of something; a fundamental truth, law; that which gives substance its essential qualities.* And yes, it would seem that Principle is Law, by this definition. But Law is not Principle, because Law is not the ultimate source, origin, or cause of something. Only Principle is. If we are to believe that harmony and orderliness prevail throughout the universe, then we must also attribute it to but one ultimate source; that of Principle.

Now, what can be said about Principle, other than as defined?   Try this: From a philosophical standpoint, Principle can be defined as being the *essence* of a unity consisting of the *coexistence* of ultimate *Truth* and *Law* ...neither of which can exist without the other... in the sense that Truth is the *source,* the origin of everything that "is," whereas Law is the ultimate basis or *cause* responsible for effecting the essence of the Truth of what "is." Again, I'll explain:

By nature, Truth is *subjective,* in that it is aware of itself in the sense that it distinguishes itself as being the ultimate truth of what "is." And by virtue of its subjectiveness, whenever and wherever Truth encounters itself, its recognition of itself *initiates a causative action* that demands the condition be effected. Law, on the other hand, unlike Truth, is *objective;* it is totally unaware of its existence and what it does, in that because of its impartial nature (without bias), Law *acts* upon any condition occasioned by Truth, thereby effecting (making manifest) essential properties of the causative condition accordingly. In other words, *whenever Truth encounters a truth, it evokes or occasions a condition, whereupon Law acts upon it impartially by giving the condition its substance and essential qualities* ...i.e., a rose becomes a rose whenever the conditions of what a rose is is recognized by Truth and subsequently effected into being by the action of Law acting upon it. In effect, then, Principle is the essence of what Truth and Law represent as a unity. And for being all of that, I think "Principle" rates the recognition it deserves, that's why I choose to give it a capital "P". Again, Principle is the essence of the omnipotent presence of Truth and Law at work throughout the universe.

So where am I going with this? Hang on! It should make some sense in just a moment.

A PRINCIPLED MEDIUM

I know that for most of us its difficult to comprehend the expanse of the universe. We know it's big. But in spite of the fact we speak of billions of light years, etc., in spite of the fact we are told the universe is infinite, chances are most of us still conceptualize the universe in terms of three-dimensional form and shape. We conceive of it as an almost unimaginable amount of space in the shape of a sphere wherein everything takes place. In short, we think of the universe in the same terms we think of living in a house; something in which other things reside within. Well, it's true we reside within a house and the house resides within the universe. But what of the universe, what does it reside within? Or is it the ultimate; there being nothing enveloping the universe? Let's take a look.

Consider, if you will, what happens when you plant something in a pot of fertile soil versus depositing a similar seed upon a concrete slab. In terms of what you hopefully understand about Principle so far, does the seed placed on the concrete slab grow and become a plant the same as the seed planted in the pot does? Of course not. Why not? Simply because of the Truth aspect of Principle pertaining to the growing of plants, certain conditions of Truth must be met and occasioned in order to bring about predictable result: plants grow when planted in fertile soil, not on slabs of concrete. Okay? Well, what if the particular Truth aspect pertaining to the planting of seeds did not exist? What then? Would the seed produce a plant? Would there be a seed to plant in the first place? But of course not! Everything that is, is so by virtue of Principle. Everything has its origin, its basis, its substance because of Principle ...the essence of ultimate Truth and Law. Without the presence of the other, there can be no Truth or Law; there can be no condition of Cause and Effect; there can be no harmony and orderliness;

and there can be no substance and essential properties. There can be nothing!

Okay. If I made my point, you should now understand that nothing can exist outside the presence of Principle (Truth and Law). Meaning the universe must exist within the influence of Principle because before there can be anything effected anywhere there needs to be a presence of origin, an ultimate basis or cause, fundamental Truth and Law, and a source which gives substance its essential properties, i.e., there must be a presence of Principle. And so there must be. Principle would have had to be already in effect before the creation of the universe took place ...as there must be in the case of the Creation theory. And in order for its creation to become manifest, the universe had to evolve "within" something in the same sense that a plant evolves from a seed planted "within" a pot of fertile soil (as opposed to a concrete slab). In this sense, then, at least to our finite brain systems, the universe (and everything in it) can be regarded as having evolved in a sort of infinite "pot of fertile soil," or better yet, an incorporeal (immaterial) "Principled Medium" wherein everything, including paranormal phenomena, evolves and has its being. In other words, if you regard the extent of the universe as analogous to an incorporeal fertile garden wherein anything and everything is effected in accordance with some particular aspect of Truth invoked, you should have a working-concept of the Medium of which I speak; that everything has its being in a Principled Medium.

Now let's draw a few conclusions about the conditions pertaining to the Medium. Because of the fact that a state of harmony and orderliness is sustained throughout the universe, it is only logical to assume, then, that everything within the Medium exists as it does by virtue of the consistency of an omnipresence of Principle, in that a tree is an effected condition of a tree because it meets the Truth aspects of what a tree is, just as a rock, electricity, a book, a hammer, a blade of grass, a speck of dust, you, your dog or cat, your thoughts, your behavior, ad infinitum, meet the conditions of the Truth of what they are. This being the case then, since everything exists by virtue of a Principled Medium and in turn occasions, responds, and effects Principle accordingly, it would mean that *nothing takes place in the universe by chance* (in the sense that Truth and Law is not involved); that everything is both affected and effected according to Principle no matter how bizarre the event, condition or situation may be so long as Truth and Law are present. With this in mind we can now attempt to synthesize how it is possible for the various phenomena discussed earlier was able to take place.

INTUITION

Let's begin with Cleave Baxter's experiment with plants. How was it possible for the philodendron plant to sense Baxter's thoughts, and Baxter's polygraph, in turn, to record the plant's reaction? As I see it, it's a case of communication exchanged within a Principled Medium. When Baxter was contemplating burning the philodendron's leaf, his thoughts (because he has his being in the Medium) made an impression upon it, whereupon the philodendron (also having its being in the Medium, and by virtue of its intuitive nature of being "attuned" to it) perceived Baxter's thought and responded accordingly as evidenced by Baxter's polygraph attached to the plant. Could it be that Principle, per se, accounts for this? Could it be that it is responsible for a possible "synthesized" intuitive communication between different forms of life including Principle, itself? Is it because of such a possibility that fish, birds and animals are able to navigate with pin-point accuracy? And is it because of the presence of Principle and their intuitiveness that lost dogs and cats are able to travel hundreds of miles over unfamiliar territory and locate their masters? How about the case of the youngster with "beginner's luck;" in spite of the expertise of his father, could it be that the fish the boy caught were only responding to his strong thoughtful anticipations impressed upon the Medium? That's how I see it, and equally so insofar as the telepathy, dowsing, premonition and intuitive episodes except for one difference; in the case of dowsing, I believe that "dowsers" *purposely* "attune" their intuitive sensor to the Medium in order to align themselves with the transmissions of that which they are dowsing for. Telepathy involves essentially the same conditions; the receiver has to *purposely* attune his/her intuitive sensor to the Medium in order to receive the impressions occasioned by the sender. Cases of premonition and intuition are essentially the same in this regard, too, except that the receiver is not necessarily purposely attuned to the Medium, but being a part of it is somehow intuitively tuned in (receptive) nevertheless.

In the case of Edison's inventions, Mozart's early compositions, and the like, I believe that their "inspirations" came to them from the Medium, in that the principles of Edison's inventions were in existence when Moses was in the Sinai Desert as were they for the compositions of Mozart. By purposely or accidentally attuning their intuitive sensors to the Medium they apparently extracted the knowledge they were seeking (just as I believe any one of us can do should we so desire). If this be the case, it strongly suggests the Medium can be regarded as a source of certain knowledge we might be seeking.

As for the likes of Edison and Mozart, whenever I experience the kind of talent displayed by them I strongly suspect that the talent, per se, is a carry-over from other lives lived, as would also be the case of Taylor Caldwell, Emerson and others. I think it's a case of ...the fact that we *have* our being in the Medium, we add to the Medium much in the same way our experiences add to our memory systems... a record of experiences exists in the Medium of which can be referenced by any one who learns to communicate intelligently with It. This would also give credence for the possibility that the Medium serves as a conduit for extra-incorporeal perception and travel, as in the case of the likes of Edgar Cacye and Pat Price. Apparently by intuitively attuning themselves to the Medium in some special way they can effectively experience out-of-body experiences and distant viewing. As for Peter Hurkos's ability to describe happenings in detail that had already taken place, such as a kidnapping or murder, he, too, undoubtedly picked up this information from the Medium by intuitively attuning himself to it, keeping in mind, of course, that everything that was, is now, and will be, seemingly exists as an indelible record in the Medium.

And then there is the case of where the Medium serves as a conduit for tapping and occasioning energy or possible "life-force" as exerted and utilized by the likes of Dr. Olga Worral and Nelya Mikailova. Like all of those who display an ability to effect paranormal phenomena, these people apparently align themselves with possible force fields of the Medium and use their Principle-given (or God-given, if you prefer) "talents" to produce the effects they do.

So what kind of conclusions can we draw regarding the Principled Medium? I mean, it seems to be a "something" for everything; a medium where everything has its being, serves as a communication exchange, a source of knowledge, a conduit for occasioning and utilizing energy, a means for apparent "out of body" experiences, distant viewing ...past, present and future, and so on. We know it exists because we apparently have our being within it. But it's incorporeal; we can't see it or touch it. Yet, as the evidence seems to indicate, by purposely aligning one's self with it, it can be purposefully utilized.

Let's face it. We're involved in a dimension whereby anything and everything is possible wherein the scope of Truth and Law of Principle exists. As mentioned earlier, science has advanced to the point where the whole and the parts of the universe is viewed as consisting of matter and energy; that matter and energy is like but two sides of the same coin; the coin being of the same substance as both its sides, but the sides taking on different manifestations. In the case of manifestation of matter, science has come to see all material things, including bone, flesh and tissue of the human body as not being solid, but rather as a collection of the substance which accounts for matter and energy (atoms); that when a particular manifestation of atoms combine into a variety of visible forms, we are seeing these visible forms as matter, and when a particular manifestations of atoms combine into a variety of invisible forms, although they are not seen, they do in fact exist, but in forms of energy. The Medium, then, exists as a dimension in the same sense as the energy side of the coin we don't see.

Now if all of this seems far out to you (as I'm sure it does), I would like you to consider this: It wasn't too long ago ...prior to the advent of the telegraph... that anyone who would have suggested the possibility of wireless communication, such as radio and TV, would have been laughed out of town. Today we know better. We know there are signals ...electro-magnetic waves, to be exact... (invisible forms of energy that do in fact exist) that leave some far away broadcasting station here on earth as well as the outer edge of our solar system, carrying sound and pictures that somehow wind-up in our living rooms. Yet no one has ever seen those waves (of energy) that produce sound and pictures; we have only seen their *effect*. Well, what's so different about the intuitive phenomena we have been discussing and what every school kid takes for granted today? Frankly I see no difference. If it is possible to purposely send a wave of energy from earth to activate a switch on a space probe trillions of miles in space, it is certainly possible for a psychokinesis medium from Russia to purposely utilize the energy of the same Medium in separating the white from the yoke of a raw egg from six feet away, or for a plant, fish, animal or telepathic receiver to purposely receive the thought transmissions (a form of energy) of someone or something else, as was the case of the duck responding to the demise of her ducklings in a submarine hundreds of miles away. It's all just a matter of being intuitively "attuned" to a Principled Medium; a possibility that is available to anyone who chooses to pursue it because each of us is an integral part of it.

Okay. Thank you for your patience. If you think that was tough to read. You should have been around when I was trying to put it down in words. Anyway, I think you will find it helpful in what's to follow.

PSYCHOLOGY OF GOALS

Dreams are the seedlings of reality. Whatsoever can be inwardly conceived can be outwardly experienced.

As you will come to realize, the achievement of goals ...material or otherwise... is not the result of happenstance, wishful thinking or hard work. To the contrary, the accomplishment of goals is dependent upon a number of factors which heretofore have been little understood. Once you are aware of what they are and how they can be brought into play, the attainment of all goals should take on a new meaning for you, both in terms of making their acquisition that much easier and in your selection of them as to scope and quality.

Goals, as the term applies here, is any objective considered worthy of achievement, all of which can be classified in one of three categories: First, there are goals, personal in nature, wherein the objective is to improve one's Self, as discussed in a previous chapter. Second, there are goals, material in nature, wherein the objective is to acquire material needs usually realized as a result of self improvement, such as a new car, a home, clothes, a trip abroad, etc. And third, there are goals of ambition ...personal or materialistic... which can be considered tantamount to reaching for the moon, but which are obtainable never-the-less. It is goals of this nature we will be considering here, because they, by far, typify the precept of what this book is all about: that *anyone* can make things happen in their life as they want them to be; not by effort, not by hard work, but through the proper application of thought.

Let me give you an example of the kind of goals I'm referring to. Let's assume you're on a fixed annual salary and barely making ends meet. You have a spark of ambition, you're loaded with confidence, you want to double your income, but not in the conventional way, i.e., putting in your time with the company, taking the normal promotions, generally going along with the system, but you want to at least double your income in a year! Is that ambitious or what?

Obviously, if you're just barely getting by now and you want to double your income in a year's time, something about your present approach to life is going to have to change. But what? Are you going to change things by going back to school in hopes the additional education is going to demand a raise in salary? Perhaps. But double what it is now? Are you going to work harder assuming you're giving it your best shot now? Are you going to put in more than the ten or twelve hours on the job you are presently doing? And even if you do these things, is a year of burning the candle at both ends going to convince the boss you're worth double your present salary? There's always that possibility, of course. But the chances of doubling your salary under these circumstances are too remote to even consider. What you really need is help ...all you can get! And assuming you don't marry the boss's daughter, it's going to have to come from some source you haven't yet found the combination to. Can you guess what it might be? Right! It has to do with learning to utilize the potential that lies waiting for you in the Principled Medium. Before we get into that, however, let's take a look at the kind of planning you should do for making your ambitious goals a reality.

Actually, the procedure is much the same as that suggested for the attainment of Personal goals. There are a few points you should be aware of, however. One is that goals should always be harmonious with one another. For example, if you have the desire to become President of the company you work for and you are aware of the limited earnings this will entail, you shouldn't set an additional goal of income that is beyond the means of the President's salary, because it would conflict with that of becoming President. Should you do so, you would likely prevent either from happening.

Another suggestion is to always set your goals high enough to be worthy of challenge. They should be set so they are just within the realm of possibility; something you know is going to take some doing to achieve. Too often people make the mistake of wanting things that are either too far beyond their reach or too easy to achieve to be considered ambitious at all. Goals that are challenging are actually easier to attain than those you feel are just a matter of time. Don't waste your time or effort on penny-ante stuff; go for the big ones, the ones which promise the greatest rewards.

With this in mind, get out some paper and list as many goals as you think you would like to see become a part of your life ...making sure they are harmonious with one another and that they are high enough to be in keeping with the affirmations you made in the part of your plan dealing with personal goals. Once listed, write a statement about each goal as to (1) why you want it, and (2) the good you expect to gain in receiving it.

Once completed, select three of the most important goals from the list and set the others aside. Take the first of the three and write a description of it in detail. For example, if it is an expensive home you want, try to describe it in every possible detail you can think of ...style of architecture, floor plan, the pitch of the roof, material used, exterior features, interior features, cabinets, floor covering, and so on. If you happen to run across a picture in a magazine which expresses the feeling of what you want, cut it out and put it in a scrap book. The more detail, the better the picture of it will be in your mind. If your goal happens to be an expensive car or boat, do the same thing; detail it from every aspect possible.

Treat each of your three goals in the same manner ...detail! detail! and more detail!

The reason for this is simple. In spite of what you may think, if you are presently suffering from the lack of things you desire in life, it is not a case of your not being worthy or that you lack the ability. It is more than likely because you have been vague in expressing your desires to yourself (your brain), vague in your belief that you are deserving, vague in your ability to produce it, and vague that it will ever become manifest. Your brain system, like a computer, responds and carries out its function in direct accordance to the data made available to it. If you impress it with data vague in nature, so will be the results produced by it. Remember the computerese expression: GIGO (garbage in garbage out)? It's the same deal. That's why all the detail. The more detail conjured up by your imagination, the greater will be its impact upon your memory. The greater the impact, the more reason it has for achieving it. Detail is essential! Okay?

Once completed, write out a simple statement of affirmation about each. For example, if one of your goals is to own a Lear Jet, write out an affirmation something like this: **"I** (or if you happen to be a family...We) **always enjoy flying in my** (our) **Lear Jet!"** If your goals is to own a sail boat, write, **"I am having a ball sailing in my Cal 40!"** If your goal is to double your income, write, **"It's a great delight to deposit \$\$\$\$\$\$ in my account every year."** Be as specific as possible. Keep your affirmations simple and always in the present tense, and always with the inference that they *have already been realized.*

In the case of your Personal affirmations, it was suggested you reduce them to a simple key word and to list them on a card as something to refer to during the course of the day. In place of this, try to find pictures which best describe your particular goals, making sure they are small enough to carry around in your wallet or purse. In referring to them often their content will become upper most in your Conscious further reminding it to make it a part of your life right now!

As always, don't talk about your affirmation with others unless they are directly involved in what you are doing, otherwise you subject yourself to too much negative feedback. Keep your personal affirmations to yourself. But if you are married, certainly involve your spouse when it comes to material goals. Interestingly enough, and for reasons which will become obvious to you later on, with two of you practicing the same affirmations, the speed with which they are attained is much more rapid than in the case of one person working alone; with two brains impressing the Medium with like or similar data, it commands a greater affect than a single brain working alone. More on that later.

Okay. Now let's turn our attention to the theory behind effecting ambitious goals in the Medium. If you recall from what you just read (hopefully) in the last chapter, Truth *initiates* a condition of what's to be effected, while Law, in turn, *effects* it into being. It was also said that Truth is subjective; in that it is aware of itself in terms of what it is and what it isn't, and that by virtue of Its subjectivity, whenever Truth encounters a like Truth, *its recognition that it is Truth* is what initiates the condition. Well, that's how it is possible for you or anyone else to double your income within a year; you're going to occasion Truth to initiate a condition of your choosing while confidently knowing that Law will effect it for you.

As you should know by now, all is Principle; everything *is* and *becomes* because of some variation of Principle. Meaning, there is some applicable principle out there in the Medium that can and will effect your goals for you. You should also know that the established condition of what a principle represents is defined by some specific Truth, and that the principle will not be effected until those conditions are met. In case you're wondering, the reason for not capitalizing principle as I'm using it here, is because I'm referring to a specific principle; a principle that's a part of Principle, not Principle, itself. Okay?

No matter the nature of your goals, you should consider your objective as analogous to valuables stored in a safe-deposit box somewhere in the Medium (you know, the ones that require two keys to open?), in that your objective does, in Principle, already exist, but in order to realize it you need to open the box. One of the keys you don't have to be concerned with is that of the "principle: involved; it's going to occasion the action when conditions in accordance with your impressions upon the Medium are met. The other key is your responsibility; you're going to have to *define the conditions* to the Medium just as you want them to be.

Now, remember the bit about Cleave Baxter "contemplating" stimulating the philodendron leaf by burning it, whereupon it responded? Well, the fundamentals involved here are essentially the same; it's a matter of *cause and effect.* When you purposely impress the Medium with thoughts of doubling your income in a year, you are, in a sense, making a strong statement of Truth that "this is how it is;" you are defining a condition of how you want things to be. In response, the principle involved will attempt to occasion an action accordingly. But you should not think you are suddenly going to have your income doubled on the spot; certain conditions will have to be met: the extra money is going to have to come from somewhere, and its going to have to be supplied by someone in need of the kind of services you are capable of rendering. Keep in mind that the cosmic state of the universe is established and sustained by the presence of Principle. This being the case, you can be assured the principle involved will recognize the Truth of both conditions, whereupon it will be initiated and subsequently effected accordingly.

WHEN PREPARATION MEETS OPPORTUNITY

Okay. Assuming you haven't married the boss's daughter and conditions have been met, then by virtue of someone's needs, plus your own, having been impressed upon the Medium, this is how it could conceivably be brought about ...not by effort, not by physical labor, but through the proper application of *purposeful* thought: In the course of mentally picturing yourself as already having doubled your income, the energized experience of your purposeful mental affirmations and contemplations will become strongly impressed upon the Medium. In response, the principle involved will become evoked, meaning it will search-out a comparable condition to the truth of your affirmation ...in this case a comparable condition impressed earlier upon the Medium by some unknown person *in need* of someone with your qualifications at double the income you are making now.

Assuming you have prepared yourself, in that you have mentally aligned or intuitively "attuned" yourself to the Medium, you will be readily receptive to any hunches, inspirations, ideas or intuitions that will, like an invisible hand, direct your inner thoughts and actions in such a way as to lead you to the eventual manifestation of what you are presently affirming. In this case, assuming the principle involved has located a match-up to your affirmations and invoked a condition of Truth, you might receive an intuitive flash to make a sales call in a part of your territory seldom visited in the past. Having made yourself receptive to the Medium (a case of being prepared when opportunity comes your way), you make the call. Finding the call productive, you complete your business and are about to excuse yourself, when out of the blue you are asked if you know of anyone with your qualifications who would like to come to work at a figure twice that of what you're making now. And of course you do! And in accepting the offer, both conditions impressed upon the Medium are fulfilled because of the principle involved

...not by luck or chance, not by coincidence, but by virtue of Principle in action: wherever there is a cause, an effect is sure to follow in direct accordance.

Undoubtedly, you have had like or similar experiences in your life. And because you were unaware of the mechanics involved at the time you no doubt assumed them to be coincidental or a stroke of good luck. Hopefully, you now know differently; you know that all is Principle; that behind every effect there has to be a cause, apparent or not. It can be no other way where harmony and orderliness prevail, as can be attested to by the following incidences:

Although the cause may not be apparent, Charles H. Wells went to Monte Carlo in 1891 with 4,000 English pounds. He played no system, placed bets on numbers all over the roulette table. The effect? He won millions. A year later he returned and did it again! Someone was so inspired by his feats that they wrote a song about him, "The Man Who Broke The Bank At Monte Carlo."

In 1919 a Romanian refugee wandered into a Paris gambling casino with only 100 franks to his name. He placed 20 franks on black. While the roulette wheel was spinning he was jostled from behind which led to a confrontation and a fight. Once settled, he returned to find his 20 frank wager had pyramided to 20,480 franks; black had come up 10 times running. His story doesn't end here by any means. Leaving France, he went to America where he became fond of bridge. He wrote a book about it. Perhaps you have heard of him ...Ely Culbertson?

After the Revolutionary War, a New Englander, Timothy Dexter "foolishly" bought baskets full of "not-worth-a-continental" paper currency for a song. A year later Alexander Hamilton stabilized the nation's economy and redeemed the old currency. With this new wealth, Dexter "foolishly" purchased some 42,000 bed-warming pans and shipped them off to, of all places, the West Indies. A tropical sugar planters found them perfect for skimming molasses and sent the price soaring trying to buy them up. On another "foolish" whim, Dexter sent two more vessels to the West Indies, this time carrying cats and Bibles. The cats arrived during a sudden plague of rats, and the Bibles sold like hot cakes during the height of a religious revival. Possibly thinking the metaphor, "send coals to Newcastle" meant a chance to make big profits, Dexter, again "foolishly," dispatched a shipload of coal to Newcastle, the coal center of England. His cargo arrived during a miner's strike and it was bought-up at monopolistic prices.

Do I regard these incidences as coincidental? Not on your life! No one who gambles and wins does so believing he's going to lose. And no one buys-up currency, dispatches boat loads of goods around the world thinking he's doing something foolish, either. Whatever the degree of effect produced, it is always directly related to the nature of the causative action responsible for it. It's strictly a matter of Principle: As you choose to believe, so it shall be for you. It can be no other way!

Until the time comes when we learn to use our brain consciously and constructively, we shall be using it unconsciously and possibly destructively. With few exceptions, this is precisely what most of us have been doing all along. Unaware of the affect it is having upon our lives, we have been unconsciously programming our brains with negative and restrictive information, and we have been unconsciously impressing the Medium with equally negative and destructive expressions. We have been literally making our lives miserable because we have been too ignorant to know how to make them otherwise. Hopefully, that is about to change as a result of learning to make the most of your potential through the constructive use of the Medium.

The fact that you have had brief flashes of intuition in the past, and the fact that clairvoyants, such as Peter Hurkos, have had frequent and lengthy experiences along this line, is indicative that communication with the incorporeal world of the Medium is a natural happening of the human experience. It is also indicative that there is much benefit to be gained from it, especially for those who learn to utilize it as a means of tapping the Truth in terms of intelligence and knowledge of Principle ...past, present, and future. For example, possibly referring to a Source of knowledge beyond the confines of his own mind, Emerson wrote that he always read his essays with great interest, and frequently found that they contained concepts and theories unfamiliar to him. Mozart, without hesitation, said that he didn't feel he really composed music at all, but rather that he simply listened and wrote down the music he heard. Thomas Edison noted that all of his important inventions came to him in full-blown inspirations, complete in every detail. Robert Louis Stevenson claimed the "brownies" helped him write his stories, meaning, of course, it seemed as though something outside of himself helped him in his writing.

These are not isolated cases by any means; literature is literally peppered with reports of people of accomplishment who give credit or mention to "something" outside themselves as being responsible for their deeds. To me, the source of this recognition is no mystery; it is indicative that, either knowingly or by some prescient act they were unaware of at the time, these individuals were intuitively making constructive use of a common channel, frequency or link of the Medium which put them in touch with the ultimate source; that of Truth. And the fact that each of us has had brief encounters with Truth before is more than evident that by learning to properly communicate with the Medium, it is possible to discover and constructively utilize much of the potential that lies somewhere in the Medium and incorporate it in turning our needs and desires into reality.

Okay. In that it has been suggested that our potential lies within the incorporeal Medium, it would seem, then, that the only way in which it can be constructively used on a corporeal level is by allowing "it" to work *through* us, which is possible only if we provide a receptive pathway or link over or through which it can flow. So, in other words, if we don't purposely make the effort to provide the means and the way to open-up two-way communication with the Medium, we are denying ourselves of a great opportunity to utilize the potential that awaits us.

Pathway? Receptiveness? What are we talking about? Let me give you an example: Suppose you were having a tough time finding a solution to a problem, and you decided to take a stab at tapping the Medium for the answer. In order for the solution to be made known to you, you would have to be receptive to the Medium on a regular basis. And in order to do that, it would be necessary to "attune" yourself or provide a pathway of communication over which the solution could be revealed to you. Such is precisely why it is possible for psychics and clairvoyants to do what they do; whether purposely or inadvertently, they seem to be able to "tap" the potential of the Medium because they have provided a receptive pathway by which it can intuitively flow through them.

Potentially, our potential is there in the Medium to be utilized in any way we may so desire. But it will do us no good at all until we learn to provide a receptive path or channel by which it can work through us. And the only way we can do that is by learning to intuitively attune ourselves to the frequency that ties us to the another dimensioned world of Principled Medium. Fortunately, such a state of receptiveness can be achieved by anyone desiring to do so by purposely altering one's state of mental awareness; a state which can be self-induced at any place, at any time.

THE ALPHA STATE

When we speak of a mental state of awareness, it is generally thought to mean either that of being asleep, or awake (conscious, or unconscious). Such is not the case, however. Science has done much research along this line, and it seems they have discovered that there is more to mental awareness than just that of consciousness or unconsciousness.

With the aid of an electroencephalograph (EEG) machine, it has been established that the brain emits essentially four distinct wave-form patterns which are associated with specific states of mental awareness. They are as follows: (1) Beta waves which indicate a state of wakefulness, (2) Alpha waves which indicate what could best be described as the "twilight zone" that lies between the state of wakefulness and sleep, (3) Theta waves which indicate a state of undisturbed sleep and (4) Delta waves which are an indication of total unconsciousness. (In the operating room, by administering certain drugs, the anesthesiologist can easily put the patient into any of these states, depending upon the type of operation.)

Probably the most rewarding discovery made about Alpha was turned up while conducting experiments associated with the state of sleep (Theta). It seems that although each of us passes through all four states of mental awareness in the course of a 24-hour period, the occurrence of Alpha, in particular, takes place at what could be considered a most opportune time, especially when one considers the significance of what the Alpha state means in terms of mind control. Specifically, I am referring to the fact that the Alpha state occurs "naturally" just prior to dropping-off to sleep at night, and prior to awakening in the morning. It also occurs intermittently throughout the "wakeful" state of Beta ...often referred to as a state of "day-dreaming."

In that the Alpha state occurs naturally in the human experience, it is my strong belief that its source is inherently rooted in the earlier stages of our brain development, going back, possibly, as far as earliest evolvement of the brain stem ...the Medulla Obligonta. My reasoning for this stems from the fact that all of life appears to be naturally attuned to the Medium on a trans-receiving basis, in that, as discovered by Cleve Baxter, plants and animals are receptive to man's thoughts, just as man, in many cases, is equally receptive to plant and animal transmissions. As I see it, the only explanation for this phenomena is that, by Nature. ...that is, biological evolution... all of life possesses the capacity to communicate with one another by virtue of an inherent two-way link with the Medium.

In the case of plants and animals, I believe this inherent link remains quite strong. Whereas in the case of man, although we possess the capacity, our receptive side of the link, generally, is somewhat diminished due to lack of use and/or our ignorance that we possess it. We are not directly to blame, however. Nature had a lot to do with it. You see, every landscape throughout the world reflects wondrous adaptations by organisms to an environment ...the butterfly which mimics leaves, the fish which appears to be something it is not, an animal's stripes and camouflage which blend in with its surroundings... all of this has been brought about by millions of years of evolution. But Nature for some unexplained reason did not provided you and I with such devices. And yet ...and this is the paradox of the human condition as opposed to all other living things... lacking such devices, we, unlike all the other inventions of Nature, are not locked into any specific landscape or environment. What devices Nature gave us are more subtle. Presumably, due to our large newer brain, nature gave us imagination, reason and toughness of mind by which we are not required to adapt to any specific environment, but to change it! And it could possibly be because of this subtlety and the mental dexterity required to survive the multitude of hostile environments ...as we have so successfully done in the past... that we have failed to recognize, discover, or utilize our link with the primal of our being, the Medium.

Whatever the reason, however, I do believe we all possess an inherent means and way to tap and utilize the great potential that lies waiting for us in the Medium, and that it can be done so purposefully through the proper application of employing the Alpha state.

I think the most obvious attribute of coming to know and utilize this inherent capacity lies in the fact that it is at the Alpha level of mental awareness where all the "necessary forces" involved in making things happen seem to be brought together; where the Principle of all that is and the incorporeal aspects of human kind can come together and communicate on a one-on-one basis. Like being in the presence of one's God, it presents an opportunity to be "heard" as well as to make "demands."

At such a level the setting, above all, is sublime; both conscious and subconscious aspects of one's brain seem to shed their differences and take on the condition of becoming one with Principle; a condition where one is better able to initiate ideas upon both the receptiveness of their own system and that of the Medium. In turn, one also becomes more receptive to the ideas and suggestions stemming from the Medium, thus resulting in better communication all around, in that that which is expressed on both sides of the threshold has a better chance of being accepted and acted upon in both dimensions.

Okay. Now it's time to consider how all of this can be employed in a beneficial way in making your life more meaningful.

MAKE IT HAPPEN

Whatsoever can be inwardly conceived can be outwardly experienced.

Purposefully attempting to reach the Alpha level is much like that of descending a ladder into a bottomless pit. Once you begin to mentally descend downward, the outside noises and activity associated with the surface begin to have less and less attraction to your conscious awareness. As a consequence, your Conscious begins to focus its attention upon what is taking place within. In a short time, you have its complete attention, and although still aware of outside activity your brain becomes more-so discerned with itself. Before long, you'll find yourself very much aware of yourself ...just you and your brain meeting face-to-face with no outside distractions to bother you. Your feeling is that of complete calmness. You're not tired or sleepy. Time and space seem to have no dimension. You are at peace with yourself and everything around you. Above all, you have the feeling that both you and your brain are completely relaxed and attentive. Once this point is reached, you are at an ideal level of mental awareness: making it possible to effectively communicate with both the Medium and yourself.

Actually, the most beneficial level of the Alpha state, insofar as communicating with the Medium, is at a point closest to the sleep state of Theta. With a little practice, you'll find this level easy to achieve and maintain. After spending a little time at this level, once you bring yourself out and back to the Beta state, you will feel more refreshed and full of energy than you have ever felt in your life before. We'll have more to say about this later.

Okay. Suppose we make a trial run at "purposefully" bringing about the Alpha state. By the way, if you were raised on television, it's quite likely you might have a little trouble mentally projecting pictures on your mental screen. Don't be concerned. It's because TV has, in a sense, robbed you of the extensive use of your imagination as is required when reading books and listening to drama being played out on the radio. Just stick with what's to follow; your brain will cooperate.

The first thing to do is to find a place of quiet where you won't be disturbed. Find a comfortable chair. Sit with hands lying across your thighs and your feet flat on the floor. Once comfortable, take a deep breath and exhale slowly. While exhaling, mentally flash a big **5** on and off on your mental screen.

While sitting there relaxed, lift your eyes up until it seems like you're looking at the underside of your eyebrows while trying to focus them on a spot on the ceiling. Hold that eye position (strained) until the eyes become so tired you feel that you would like to close them. When you do, close them, letting it happen gently and at the same time (with eyes closed) mentally picture a big **4** flashing on and off.

After a few moments of this, change the picture on your mental screen to that of seeing the top of your head while at the same time superimposing a big flashing (on and off) **3** over this scene. While this action is taking place, try to picture and feel the action of the skin of your scalp relaxing; feel the relaxing sensation spreading out and down. When the feeling gets down to your ears, feel them starting to relax in the same way ...like melted butter spreading out and running down over a stack of pancakes. Now apply this same spreading, relaxing feeling to your forehead, then your jaws, then your tongue, your throat, neck, shoulders, chest (all the while superimposing the flashing **3** on your mental screen), your back, arms, hands and fingers. Now think of your stomach and other organs relaxing. Follow this with the relaxing of your hips, your thighs, knees, calves, and finally your feet and toes. You should feel so relaxed at this point that you have no sensation of any dimension to your body. If you don't have this feeling, it is suggested you start over again, going through the same sequences described, until you can bring yourself to the point where you have no sensation of dimension to your body (when you are aware of it, but there's no conscious awareness of the outlines of the various parts).

Chances are, if you have never tried like or similar experiments before, you will find yourself being distracted by an insatiable desire to swallow or scratch. It's nothing to be concerned about; it's brought about by your brain, possibly resenting "conscious you" infringing upon up-until-now its sacred territory. Don't fight it. Scratch, swallow, or whatever, and return your attention to what you're trying to do. After a few sessions of this you won't be bothered by it any more.

Once you have established a "no-dimension" feeling, try to mentally picture your brain as being all tensed-up. Now try to picture and feel it relaxing while at the same time superimposing a big flashing **2** over the picture.

Once you see and feel your brain relaxed, picture a big flashing **1** while at the same time mentally saying to yourself: **"I am now at the basic level of Alpha, a level where I have complete control over my brain system; where outside noises do not disturb me, but rather help to make me become more deeply relaxed."**

Now turn-off the flashing **1**; you are at the basic Alpha level of mental awareness. And chances are you're not going to believe it, either. You're going to think you're only kidding yourself; that aside from being relaxed you're really not at Alpha at all because you have the feeling you can open your eyes and be wide awake any time you want. Well you can! That is what is so beneficial about using Alpha as a means to control your brain system; you're always in complete control at all times. Okay, so here you are at the basic Alpha level, completely relaxed, mentally attuned to the Medium, and in complete control of your system. Now I'll tell you how to take yourself out; not that you can't do it by just opening your eyes, but how to do it in a way that will benefit you.

Mentally say to yourself: **"I am going to count from 1 to 5. At the count of 5 I will open my eyes, be wide awake, feeling fine and in perfect health. I will have no ill effects in my body."** At this point I would like to suggest that there is certain beneficial phrasing you can use while making your "out" statement. Should you have some persistent illness or disorder you would like to rid yourself of, the suggestive qualities used at this level can do much to relieve or even cure it completely. For instance, if you are susceptible to frequent colds, you could say: *"..ill effects in my body which tolerate colds!"* Or if you have poor eye sight: *"...ill effects in my vision or eye sight!"* Or in the case of persistent headaches: *"...ill effects in my head or neck; no headaches!"* And so on. This is a great opportunity to suggest such maladies away. Do it, you'll be amazed at the results. Continuing, then, after inserting the various recitals that best suit you, follow with: **"...in fact, everything about my mental and physical condition gets better and better every time I'm at this level of mental awareness."** Follow this up by starting to count: *"one"... "two"...,* mentally saying to yourself: **"coming up slowly. "..."three." "at the count of 5 I will open my eyes, be wide awake, feeling fine and in perfect health. four." "five!"** At the count of 5, and with your eyes wide open, mentally repeat to yourself: **"I am wide awake, feeling fine, and in perfect health!"**

While still on the subject, I would like to interject another suggestion: As you begin the one-to-five count-out, you should mentally try to feel the sensation of actually "coming up" from a bottomless pit. The reason for this is because your brain, being the "learning machine" it is, it must be instructed specifically at all times. Whatever you want it to accept, you must make known to it. If you want it to accept that you are coming up out of bottomless pit, you must make it known to it by impressing it with mental pictures, feeling and emotions of coming up out of a bottomless pit. The greater the detail, the greater the impression and consequent affect it will have on your mind. So when you say you are "coming up," picture and feel yourself coming up. Then, in the future, when you are making affirmations to your mind that you are becoming "more and more relaxed," "feeling fine," or whatever, your mind will be more accommodating in bringing about the condition you are affirming. It must be remembered, that when dealing with your brain, *it accepts everything impressed upon it as fact* (it's a learning machine, remember?), and the more realistic you can make your affirmation the greater the impact it will have on your system in bringing about the desired condition.

I strongly recommend that you follow the instructions of getting "into" and "out" of Alpha to the letter. You should attempt it a least a dozen times. After you have mastered it, you can then turn to the short-cut method, which will be described in a moment. In the meantime, for your information, the purpose of practicing the longer method, as suggested, is intended to condition your brain to associate the flashing numbers with the various stages of getting into and out of Alpha, in that when you mentally picture a number your system will associate it with the particular condition synonymous with the number and will automatically respond by physically altering your mental and body conditions accordingly and thus save you the trouble of instructing it to do so each time you want to initiate the Alpha state.

The great advantage of conditioning your brain to respond to the flashing numbers is that, after a short time of conditioning, it will no longer be necessary to find a place of quiet in order to get away from disturbing outside noises. You can put yourself in a state of Alpha just about any time or place you desire; night or day, sitting at your desk, riding in an elevator, while out playing a round of golf, or whatever.

All that's necessary is that you get in such a position that you are comfortable and relaxed ...standing or sitting down... and project the appropriate numbers on your mental screen.

Now for the short method: Once comfortable and relaxed, close your eyes, take a deep breath, and while exhaling, mentally repeat and visualize the number **3** flashing on and off three times. In doing so, your brain will automatically relax your body from head to toe. Now take another deep breath, and while exhaling, mentally repeat and visualize the number **2** flashing on and off three times ...signifying to your system to relax. Follow this with another deep breath, and while exhaling, mentally repeat and visualize the number **1** flashing on and off three times ...signifying to your brain that you are at the basic Alpha level. If you have mastered the longer method before attempting this shorter version, you should be able to reach the basic level within a matter of seconds ...a most desirable situation you'll find to be very beneficial, especially in terms of stress or fatigue, because you can put yourself in Alpha and relieve tension or call for a little recuperative power and be ready to meet any situation head-on in a matter of minutes.

As said before, the deeper the state of Alpha, the more receptive your system becomes, both to your suggestions and to the Medium. In order to reach the deeper levels, all you have to do is mentally say to yourself (assuming you are at the basic level) is: **"I am now at the basic Alpha level, a level where I have complete control over my system; where I am perfectly aligned with the Medium; where outside noises do not disturb me, but rather help to make me become more and more relaxed. Wishing to go to deeper levels where programming has its strongest affect upon my brain; where I have complete access to the Medium, I am going to count backwards from 10 to 1; each count down causing me to become**

more and more relaxed." Then start counting down slowly: "ten"..."nine".., mentally saying to yourself: **"I'm becoming more and more relaxed!"**... "eight"... "seven"... "six"... **"more and more relaxed."**... "five"... "four"... "three"... **"more relaxed."**... "two"... **"and one."** When finished counting, mentally say to yourself: **"I am now at a level deeper than before, a level I know my system to be the most receptive to any instructions I wish to impress upon it! A level where I am one with the Medium."**

At this level you are parked on the threshold which separates the world of your brain and that of the Medium. Conditions are ideal. At this state you literally have "the key to the candy store" in hand. You are totally in charge. The world and everything in it literally lies at your feet. This is your chance to set in motion the forces-that-be to make anything happen you may desire. You can use this opportunity to relieve tension, solve problems, effect the conditions of *others,* over-come bad habits, develop constructive habits, and realize both ambitious and personal goals.

If you will recall, it was suggested earlier that the best time to recite your affirmations is just before falling asleep and upon awakening in the morning. Now you know why; it is because this is the time when we are normally in a "natural" state of Alpha. But like trying to catch the first rays of sun every morning, it is not always possible unless conditions are ideal. To insure against this possibility it is suggested that you supplement your morning and night sessions with a once-a-day session of the Alpha state brought about purposely, say during a lunch break, or whenever you can find the fifteen or twenty minutes during your wakeful state. In that way you will be sure that conditions are as they should be.

PUTTING ALPHA TO WORK

Okay. As they say on the farm,"...it's plantin' time." Once you get yourself situated at the lower levels of Alpha it's time to start purposely impressing the Medium with mental pictures and feelings of how you want things to be. And here's a suggestion on how to go about doing it: Begin by mentally reciting the beneficial phrase, **"Day by day, in every way, everything is getting better, better, and better!"** Now try to mentally picture a curtain withdrawing across your mental screen; you are about to impress this screen with pictures and feeling of how you want things to be with the connotation that they all ready exist in your life. Make sure that the curtain is divided in the middle and that it is withdrawn to a point beyond your peripheral vision on both sides. The sole purpose of this is to give you a feeling that you are part of the action taking place on the screen ...the same feeling you have in a natural state of awareness. Were the curtain in the way, you would have the feeling you were a spectator looking at a screen (externalizing) ...the last thing in the world you want your brain to assume when programming.

With the opening beneficial statement made and the curtain withdrawn, you can begin your affirmations. Begin with the category of S E L F.

Establish the scene on your mental screen. Look! There you are, mingling with all sorts of people. Now, feel yourself as being that person (you) on the screen. And what are you doing? You're making those people *feel important,* of course! And how are you accomplishing that? You're walking around with a nice friendly *smile* on your face. Notice how the people smile back. While you *feel* (not see) yourself mingling with people (smiling and it being returned), mentally say to yourself: **"I always wear a smile!"** Try to keep the scene as realistic as possible. Notice the dresses the ladies are wearing; the mustaches or beards on the different men. Feel like you are a part of the surroundings; feel the cold highball glass in your hand, and so on. Remember, you're putting on this show for the benefit of your brain system and the Medium; the more realistic you can see it and feel it, the greater prominence it's going to have when recorded in your memory.

Now change the scene; feel yourself moving around and mixing with other people; and feel yourself showing a sincere interest in other people while mentally saying to yourself, **"I always show a sincere interest in other people!"** Keep the scenes changing. Now feel yourself face-to-face with a person who appears to be dull. Instead of excusing yourself and moving on, here's a great opportunity to see how successful you are at making people feel important. Feel yourself turning the person "on" by getting him to talk about him/herself while mentally saying, **"I always encourage others to talk about themselves!"** Think of what you are doing as like a game; the more they respond to your smile, your interest in them, your encouragement in getting them to talk about themselves, etc., the better the player you are. The more and better you play the game on your mental screen the sooner it's going to become a natural part of your daily life. When it does, you'll become an instant winner!; a winner, because you've learned to give people what they want most: *favorable recognition and appreciation.*

Shift to a new scene; that of being introduced to new faces. While this is going on, mentally brand their names across their foreheads and say to yourself, **"I always remember people's names and faces!"** Now get involved with the people you have just met. Try, for instance, to picture someone speaking argumentatively. While they are carrying on, feel yourself playing the role of the person you have affirmed yourself to be so far. And even though you'd like to tell this argumentative person a thing or two, mentally say to yourself, **"I always respect the other person's opinion!"** And when you say it, at the same time feel it and mean it. After all, when a person expresses an opinion, they are only relating the nature of the data stored in their memory ...as is the case with you, also. Besides, being right or wrong should not be an issue, because no one ever wins an argument!

Now end this particular category by seeing and feeling yourself making an exit in such a way that when you leave you have the feeling that you have made a most favorable impression upon all the characters involved; leave with the impression that, collectively, they're thinking what a warm and genuine person you are!

Having completed your self affirmations, shift locations and situations, and in the same way, work out scenes involving your F A M I L Y affirmations. Once this is covered, move on to your B U S I N E S S affirmations and do the same thing. Make your mental pictures as believable as you can ...believable that they are just as you want them to be!

Once completed, mentally bring this part of your plan to a close with the statement: **"And so it is!"** Now it's time to turn to your material and ambitious G O A L S. Mentally picture and say to yourself, *"This is my home!"*... *"boat!"*... *"car!"* or whatever; *"This is me making $$$$$$$ a year!"* See and feel whatever it is you're attempting to make happen. Mentally feel yourself totally involved with it while at the same time mentally affirming it. When you have completed your affirmations, close with the statement, **"And so it is!"** Follow this with a brief pause of receptiveness. Think of yourself as poised on the threshold separating the dimensions of matter and energy. Be prepared to be especially receptive to any hint or idea that could possibly come to you from the Medium. Mentally call upon the Medium if you must for ideas. Let the Medium know you are eagerly awaiting any suggestions or instructions it may have for you. Close with the statement, **"And so it is!"**

Now it's time to wrap things up and get out. Do it by slowly closing the curtain on your mental screen while at the same time mentally saying to yourself, **"I always think positive!"** At this point, depending upon the time of day or night, you can either take the 1-5 count, or you can just let yourself slip off into a natural state of sleep. In either case, you should always take advantage of your mental state in order to get something beneficial across to your brain. At night, having ended the session, you might say: **"I'm looking forward to tomorrow because it's going to be a pleasant and productive day!"** Or, if during the day, you might say: **"This is** *(or is going to be)* **a very pleasant and productive day!"** Whatever way you wish to go, just make sure it's positive and carries the inference that the condition *already exists.*

Okay, just a few things you should keep in mind. When in the Alpha state, try to regard it as a condition of being in the presence of the most awesome forces in the universe (the Medium and your brain) that are standing by to effect whatever it is you affirm. Keep in mind, also, that because they have this capability, it is of the utmost importance that you *be specific* in your affirmations. If you affirm a condition in general terms, money, for instance, it will surely be given unto you ...but it could be anything from pennies to millions. Don't take the chance. Be specific as to when you expect to have it and in what amount. Anything that is worthwhile is worth describing in detail, especially when it will be given unto you in accordance with how you see it and feel it on your mental screen.

Whether you choose to employ the use of "self-induced" Alpha or "natural" (morning and night) occurrences of Alpha in carrying out your affirmations, it makes no difference. Both methods are effective in producing results. Self-induced Alpha, however, is by far the more effective of the two.

And as for the use of mental imagery, itself, I would like to stress that it should never be employed with the use of will power or effort. It should, rather, always be applied in a gentle and natural manner ...much in the same manner you allow yourself to worry about something. Also, as always, when employing the use of mental imagery, you should keep in mind that whatever it is you are attempting to make happen, the results you achieve will not only be made manifest accordingly, but more importantly, that they will be made manifest to the degree that you believe that they will! In other words, you shouldn't expect positive results if you, for any reason, doubt that the results will be positive.

Well, what do you think? Knowing why you think and act as you do (your brain ...a goal seeking learning machine)... knowing what you can do to change anything in your life (making it happen), and now, knowing how it can be accomplished... can you think of any good reason why you or anyone else should ever tolerate undesirable conditions in their life again? I certainly can't. But like the adage goes, "you can lead a horse to water, but you can't make him drink," it's as true of people as it is of horses. You can tell them why, what and how. But without faith that it is so, very little good can come from it. On the chance you happen to be such a person, it should indicate just how negative the data in your memory presently is. It should also suggest that if things haven't been going well for you in the past, that maybe, just maybe, it has something to do with your mental attitude (?(. Tell you what, should you want to believe, but need a little nudge in proving to yourself that you can make things happen just by thinking about it, I suggest you try a simple experiment that should give you conclusive results within a week or ten days.

AS YOU CHOOSE TO BELIEVE

The next time you go to the market, pick-up a bunch of carrots (usually 9-12 in a bunch) *with green tops intact.* When you get them home, carefully cut-off the green tops flush with the end of each carrot. Once that's done, slice off the last half-inch of the top of each carrot and place in a paper bag, setting it aside for the moment.

Remove two saucers from the cupboard. Place a paper napkin (folded in quarters) into each of the saucers. Now pour enough water on each napkin so that it is completely saturated. Set the two saucers near a window where they'll catch some outside light. Then take two slips of paper; mark one with the letter "P" and the other with the letter "N" (to signify positive and negative) and slip them under the saucers.

Now take the paper bag containing the carrot tops, close the top of the bag and shake. In order not to show favoritism for one carrot top over another, without looking inside, remove a carrot top and place it in one of the saucers. Remove another carrot top and place it in the other saucer, and so on until you have an equal number of carrot tops placed on the wet paper napkins.

The experiment is very simple. For the next week or ten days you are going to practice a little mental imagery; you're going to prove to yourself what a little purposeful thinking can do to plants. Although it would be more beneficial to both you and the results of the experiment to use the Alpha state approach, we'll try it the simplest way possible: at least twice a day, you are to sit down and make yourself comfortable. Take a deep breath and try to relax your whole body as you slowly exhale. With eyes closed you are to project a picture of the saucer "P" and the carrot tops in it on your mental screen; not as they are now, but rather *as you want them to be* ...like they were before you cut off their tops... with long green bushy tops, while mentally saying to yourself,   **"And so it is!"** Slowly repeat this affirmation a dozen times while imagining them as *already* with long green bushy tops.

Now, mentally erase this picture and replace it with a picture of the saucer "N" and the carrots in it. As before, don't picture them as they are now, but rather as you want them to be. Instead of seeing the carrots in saucer "N" as being healthy, green bushy plants, picture them as being sickly and all shriveled up with no greenery at all; like they've been out in the sun for several weeks ...wilting and dying. As you mentally picture and feel their presence, use the same phrasing as before: **"And so it is!"** Make sure you give the carrots in each saucer an equal amount of mental imagery time. And as with all mental imagery, the more detail and emotional involvement you bring into play, the better the results are going to be.

To keep the experiment on an impartial basis, it is suggested you exchange the location of the saucers every other day while making sure the paper is always damp throughout the experiment.

Within a week you should experience some results. The carrot ends in saucer "P" should start putting out shoots, while those in saucer "N" will show hardly any change. Within 10 days, the contrast will become even more evident; all of which should do much toward convincing you that your "thoughts are things;" that there is a "universal channel of communication" that ties all of creation together, and that whenever your thoughts become impressed upon the Medium, they are in turn acted upon by Principle and made manifest accordingly.

While the carrot experiment is going on, perhaps those of you who are "big city" dwellers would like to try your hand at another experiment, more ambitious in nature, which could prove to be quite beneficial. It has to do with assuring yourself of a parking spot where, by past experience, you know it to be tough to find. Here's what you are to do: While several miles from your destination, take a deep breath and try to relax all over as you exhale. Now mentally picture (with eyes open, please!) an empty parking spot at a particular place you want to park when you arrive. While picturing it try to include as much detail and feeling as possible. Picture the bank or whatever on the corner, people walking up and down the street, traffic signals, cars going by, and, of course, an empty spot where you want to park. Now mentally see yourself pulling your car into that spot while mentally saying **"And so it is!"**

Believing in what you are affirming ...believing that it will be done accordingly... is essential to making things happen as you want them to be. The more believable you can picture the particular condition in your mind, the greater the chance it has to succeed. If you keep a record of your hits and misses, I'm sure you will be pleasantly surprised at what a little purposeful thinking can do in your life.

Okay, some final words on "making it happen." If you employ just half the amount of thought and energy you splurge when you're worrying and, instead, apply it toward thinking constructively about how you want things to be in your life, you can expect to experience positive results within a matter of a few weeks. Should you find the results less than your anticipations, however, don't blame it on the system, instead, let it serve as a reminder that there's much restrictive information in your memory yet to be over-come. And because there is, don't take this to mean that you should try harder to displace it. To the contrary, chances are it could be because you have tried too hard. If anything, you should take it easy! Think of mental imagery as a positive and constructive aspect of the same conditions employed when you worry; effortlessly allow yourself to mentally dwell upon conditions *as you want them to be* instead of all the negative aspects of how you think things *could be.*

Maybe you're not aware of it, but both positive and negative thinking are equally effective in producing results. It's just that positive thinking takes management, whereas negative thinking doesn't. That's what "making things happen" is all about; you make negative things happen when you think negative, and you make positive things happen when you think positive. The Truth and Law aspects of Principle does not discern itself with either. *There's as much truth in a negative condition as there is in a positive condition.*

The point is, since you have the freedom of choice, why not go for the positive. All it takes is a little management on your part. By consciously choosing to mentally visualize and verbalize conditions *as you want them to be,* you are displacing restrictive data in your memory just as surely as a "positive" pebble dropped into a bucket of "restrictive water" displaces an amount equal to its volume. What you are at any moment in your life is directly related to the nature of the data contained within your memory. Displace restrictive data with data of your choosing, and the point will soon be reached when you are what you are because it is how you want it to be!

You should always keep in mind that everything "is" according to Principle. When dealing with matters of the mind ...what the brain does, the principles involved are non-respector of persons, places or things; they work in accordance with Truth and Law no matter who invokes them. If, for instance, you choose, knowingly or otherwise, to believe that you can't effect the growth of carrots or provide a parking spot for yourself, so, by Principle, will it be given unto you, just as it will be given to those who choose to believe that they can. The reason is simple: The principles involved, in themselves, do not make judgments as to what (in your memory) is true or false, good or bad, can or cannot be done; they, rather, effect according to your faith that it will be done accordingly, which is different. Law is the enactment aspect of any principle; in this case the principle being whatsoever one chooses to believe, so it shall be for him or her. Therefore, any time you feel you have not received the kind of results expected from employing the use of mental imagery, it should not be construed as a breakdown in the principle involved, but rather with the degree of faith involved in which the expression is made.

There can never be a breakdown whenever Truth and Law is involved. According to Principle, when you choose to believe that something doesn't work for you, then, according to Principle it doesn't work for you, because in appearing not to work for you it is really working for you; it does so by appearing not to work by effecting the condition in accordance with your belief that it doesn't work. Get it? According to your disbelief that something doesn't work for you, the principle is really working ...by appearing not to work... according to your belief that it doesn't work. Thus is the basis of the principle of thought: as you choose to believe, so shall it be for you.

Follow your plan of action each day for a period of at least 30 days. Try to avoid thinking about the kind of progress you're making. Just let it happen. Before you know it, good things will begin happening. For the first time in your life you'll feel like you have complete control over your destiny. As a result, the information of this experience, as recorded in your memory, will automatically move your *Self concept* setting upwards. As it rises, so will your outlook of self rise with it.

It is said that faith alone can produce miracles. I ask you, what is faith other than a prominence of one kind of information over another? And what faster and better way is there to acquire faith than by you programming it into your memory?

What past experiences can do, new experiences can undo. What you are today is the result of what you experienced yesterday; what you make up your mind to experience today will determine what you will be tomorrow. Remember, if you don't control your own brain, somebody else will!

Hopefully the day will soon come when each of us comes to realize that in dealing with our brain system, Truth, Law , and Principle, that we are dealing with something that is impartial to who invokes it, what it is they want, or how much of it they desire to have; that each of us experiences precisely what it is we are contemplating; that our memory, the Medium, Principle, do not discern themselves with the nature of our objectives, but only with making it become manifest in

accordance with what has been expressed ...irrespective of
who contemplates it, what it is, or how much of it is desired!

FINAL TOUCHES

Until the time comes when we learn to use our mind consciously and constructively we shall be using it unconsciously and perhaps destructively

With all the tension and anxiety associated with our fast moving world today, to be able to completely relax brain and body at will is an assurance against early demise and all the signs leading to it, i.e., ulcers, high blood pressure, heart attack, reliance upon drugs, excessive drinking, smoking, obesity, and so on. So once you've learned to program your memory (the result of at least 12 practice sessions) to alter your brain system conditions in response to the 3 to 1 short method countdown, you will find you can pull your car off the road, or while in the privacy of your office or while out on the golf course, or during the course of a "mind-bending" business meeting, excuse yourself momentarily, go into the basic alpha level, program yourself in terms of renewed energy and mental alertness, and come out of it and carry on as refreshed as if you had a normal nights sleep.

It is entirely possible that it is this same use of alpha that is responsible for the phenomenal longevity and vigor associated with the people of Hunza Valley, up in the tricorner where Afghanistan, Tibet and Russia meet. Although their diet consists of essential minerals, apricots and whole grains, they also, from early childhood, practice profound relaxation several times a day; it not being an uncommon sight to see children and adults stop, sit down, and sink into deep relaxation for 10 to I5 minutes, and then arise renewed. If these people can live actively for 130 or so years practicing diet and relaxation, who knows, maybe you can too, at least it won't hurt you to try. All that's necessary is to take the 3 to 1 countdown. When you get to the basic alpha level, take the 10 to 1 countdown to the lower level. Once at the lower level, mentally instruct your brain *that you are going to take a deep, undisturbed sleep* for a specific period of time; *that during that time, all the cells of your brain and body will be renewed with energy, and that at the end of this period you will awaken feeling fully refreshed and in perfect health.* Then as you are awakened, visualize yourself feeling yourself fully refreshed while mentally saying to yourself, *"And so it is!"* In keeping with being specific with your brain, note the time at which you take the 3 to 1 count so that you can instruct it as to how many minutes and the exact time you expect to be awakened. Okay?

NO LONGER A PROBLEM

If there is one underlying experience common to all aspects of the human experience, it is that of facing and solving problems. In this respect, Alpha has much to offer, primarily because it can put you in touch with the Medium and because it provides the means by which your brain can penetrate otherwise inaccessible regions of its memory files where possible useful suppressed information might be held under wraps.

Problems, generally, can be classified either as those requiring an immediate solution or those requiring a longer period of time. In either case, the use of Alpha can prove to be most beneficial in helping to find the solutions.

For those problems requiring an immediate solution, it is suggested that you try the following: When you go to bed at night, leave a partially filled glass of water or beverage of your choice near your bed. At the completion of your night programming session, reach over and drink half of what's in the glass while at the same time mentally saying to yourself, **"This is all I need to do in order to find the solution to the problem I have in mind. And so it is!"** Put the glass down and let yourself slip into a natural state of sleep. In the morning, after completing your programming, drink the remaining contents in the glass while mentally repeating the statement, **"This is all I need do in order to find the solution to the problem I have in mind. And so it is!"**, and then forget about your problem. Chances are, you will either receive a flash of insight during the same day or you will awaken during the night or next morning with a vivid recollection of a dream that contains the information you need for solving your problem.

As for long range solution, the procedure is much the same. But because of what's involved, some explanation is required. Consider, if you will, the following problem facing you: Your day starts out with the realization that you have no money in your bank account, there are bills to pay, your wife needs emergency surgery, and the bank has called your loan. The fact that this information comes to your attention while in the conscious state (Beta) requires that it be dealt with consciously.

In evaluating the situation, the information turned up by your Conscious indicates that you're in a pack of trouble. Fear sets in; your imagination is triggered into action and it takes off like a wild stallion. As a result you become both physically and mentally involved in its wild speculations, having little control, if any, to do anything about it. What has taken place in your brain is this: Negative information (resulting from your imagined speculation) is impressed upon your memory, which, in turn, provides your brain with still more additional information to feed upon. Before you know it, the whole problem becomes blown out of proportion, and the only decision your Conscious can make for you in terms of your best interest it that you ought to make a run for it.

True, most of us can consciously suppress our imagination to a degree when it gets out of control, but not without suffering a considerable amount of brain system anxiety and stress. Fortunately, all of this can be avoided with the help of Alpha conditioning.

If such a problem should ever face you, the moment you come to the realization that it exists, before your imagination can get a hold of it, put yourself into deep Alpha conditioning immediately. When you get there, open up the curtain on your mental screen; set the mood by mentally saying: **"Day by day, everything is getting better, better and better!"** and proceed by imagining yourself seated at the rear of a movie theater watching a movie about to be projected on the screen. Try to visualize the movie screen as a projection screen on your mental screen. This will immediately suggest to your memory that you are detached from what is about to be projected upon it. Now, mentally visualize a *red* border around the screen and proceed to project the problem on it as you understand it to be, making sure *not to* include yourself in the problem. Study and analyze the problem as though you were an observer overseeing the problem of someone else while at the same time mentally saying to yourself, **"This is the problem. After I have studied and analyzed it, it will be a problem no more!"** Now, let your imagination run free reign. Let it run its wild course once and for all, because this is the last time it will be allowed to do so.

After your imagination has had its fling, stop the projection and mentally remove the red border from around the screen and replace it with a *white* border. Now project an image of how you want things to be once the problem has been resolved within the white border while, mentally saying to yourself, **"This is as it will be!"** Follow this by mentally zooming in on the scene so that it occupies all of your mental screen, step into the scene, and then become a part of it. Once you feel you are a part of the solution, close the curtain on your mental screen with the, **"And so it is!"** and take the 1-5 count out of Alpha. From thereon the problem should never be thought of as a problem again; instead, think of it as a "project" or goal to be achieved ...the object being that the solution will turn out to be as you want it to be! This should in turn be followed up by including the "project" in your programming sessions. You should treat the "project" just as you would a material goal: isolate the project on your mental screen, making sure it is bordered by a white line; visualize it in detail and feeling while mentally saying, **"And so it is!"**

Should the so-called problem (which is not a problem anymore) ever crop-up in your brain again, it's not necessary to go into Alpha, just consciously say to yourself **"Cancel!" "Cancel!"** Then replace the negative picture or thought with a picture of the "project" while mentally saying, **"And so it is!"**

If you think this solution seems overly simplified compared to the nature of the problem, let me say this: Whether you wish to reach for a cup of coffee or you happen to find yourself up a creek without a paddle, both conditions present a problem to your brain. Each is treated by your system in the exact same way, requiring an *evaluation* using the only information available to it in the memory. If you don't make an effort to indicate to your brain just how you want things to be resolved, you are inadvertently telling it to handle the problem the best way it can, which, depending upon the nature of your fears (based on past experiences), could cause you much undue distress ...for some, even to the point of taking their own lives (which, incidentally, has led me to believe that the desire for recognition and appreciation is an even-more-so inherent trait than that of survival).

As you will find in working with your brain in the future, it cannot be harassed or forced into anything, because if you do it will rebel. In all cases of dealing with your brain it should be dealt with much as you would with a child that has a problem; it should be approached with understanding, gentleness and patience, yet you must be firm and specific and at the same time gentle. Once you win its confidence you will find its loyalty unsurpassed.

EFFECTIVENESS OF PRAYER

Another aspect of Alpha worthy of consideration is that of making things happen from a distance. The fact that at the Alpha level you are strongly aligned with the Medium, it is literally possible to contact and communicate with just about anything without being limited to time, space or dimension. Meaning, especially in the case of people, it is possible to plant suggestive information in *their* memory no matter where *they* are and have them respond to it accordingly (as mentioned in an earlier chapter). As a matter of fact, without realizing it, it is being done by people like you and me every day. For example, how many times have you heard the old story of some loved one or close friend on the verge of dying, who, after recovery, reported they sensed the presence of others' prayers, felt a renewed strength and an over-powering desire to live? The reports are innumerable. What is this other than a case of planting suggestive information in the memory of someone from a distance? Suppose we examine how this is possible.

First, let's consider the condition of the loved one or friend who is ill. Generally, due to their physical condition (coma or unconsciousness) they are emitting low frequency brain waves comparable to those produced at the Alpha or lower levels, thereby "naturally" attuning themselves to the incorporeal world of the Medium. Without realizing it, primarily because we have gathered our thoughts and focused them upon a single objective (of the patient as fully recovered), those of us who pray tend to alter our state of mental awareness sufficient enough to lower our brain wave activity to levels of upper Alpha, which in turn makes it possible for the mental pictures of the conditions as we want them to be to be picked up by the Medium. Once impressed upon the Medium, the principle involved, then, acts upon the conditions as defined by the prayers, thus working in behalf of the person intended. This, of course, is made possible by virtue of the patient's assumed state of mental awareness (either that of Alpha, Theta or Delta), in that the patient is in a natural alignment to receive them and the data being impressed on his/her memory. Once impressed upon the memory of the patient, and depending upon the prominence of the information, the patient's brain system will in turn deal with the necessary body cells and functions needed to bring about the reality in terms of its physical equivalent. In other words, through the act of prayer at the Alpha level or lower it is possible to impress information upon another's memory from a distance provided the individual's mental state of awareness is at a level receptive to receiving it ...at Alpha or lower levels.

Along this same line, I recently had a chance to see this so-called phenomena work in bettering a family's relationships. The sister of one of the students in a class I was attending on "mind control" was having trouble with her young son as a result of a divorce. It seems the child was "down" on his mother and didn't mind telling her how much he despised her because his father was no longer around. Realizing that people are normally in or close to the alpha state roughly 30 to 40 minutes before awakening in the morning, the student decided to make a stab at altering her nephew's bad behavior by planting some constructive suggestions in his brain without him knowing of it. Arising earlier than normal in order to compensate for the time difference between California and Ohio, every morning she put herself into deep Alpha level. Projecting her nephew on her mental screen, she went to work on him defining his behavior as she thought it should be. Her sister, of course, was not informed of her plans. Approximately two weeks later, I was shown a letter from the student's sister relating the "amazing" change that had taken place in her son.

Equally impressive, as related to me by the instructor of the course mentioned, was an incident involving the control of a female dog who had the nasty habit of making brown spots and leaving good sized "goodies" on peoples' lawns in the neighborhood. By going into Alpha and projecting the dog on his mental screen and visualizing her avoiding his lawn like it was loaded with pepper, the instructor conveniently eliminated an aggravating problem and at the same time maintained a pleasant neighborly relationship with the owner of the dog.

Again, should you be wondering why it is that humans are required to reach an Alpha level or lower in order to be receptive to the Medium, whereas plants and animals don't seem to be? Like I said before, I'm not sure, unless it's because animals having a smaller brain and plants having whatever (?) are less involved in the mental processing that humans have to contend with and as a consequence are less distracted and more naturally attune to the medium than we are. Maybe we'll find out one of these days. And should you entertain the fear that you might "screw-up" your brain or become addicted from using Alpha, forget it! The Alpha state of mental awareness is a "natural" function of the human experience, and if you can find a way to become addicted because of its use, I guarantee you'll become the envy of every Guru, Lama and student of meditation that ever attempted to find his/her true inner-self.

In light of what has been said of Alpha, you're probably wondering why it, in particular, seems to be so beneficial in the use of mind control. I'm sure there are a number of explanations, but I think its most obvious attribute lies in the fact that it is at the Alpha level of mental awareness where all of the necessary forces involved in making things happen are brought together; where both the energy and material sides of humankind come face-to-face in the presence of Principle (Truth and Law), thus making it possible for one-and-all to communicate at one common level.

At such a level, the setting, above all, is sublime; the brain is "as one" with Principle and the Medium. In such a state, each of us is better able to initiate our ideas both upon our respective memories and that of the Medium, and in turn become more receptive to both ourselves and the Truth of what is. The result is better communication all around, and that which is expressed on both sides of the threshold separating the incorporeal and the material dimensions has a better chance of being accepted and acted upon in both.

So much for the philosophical viewpoint. Scientifically there is a very good reason why Alpha is so beneficial; it has to do with the emission of energy. As mentioned before, in measuring brain wave emissions, each wave type produces a different frequency. Beta ...the wakeful state... produces waves that vary in frequency from a low of approximately 14 cps (cycles per second) to over 100 cps. Alpha, the so-called twilight zone between consciousness and sleep, produces waves that vary in frequency from a high of 14 cps to a low of approximately 7 cps. Theta, the sleep state, produces wave frequencies varying from a high of 7 cps to a low of 4 cps. And Delta, the unconscious state, produces waves that vary in frequency from a high of 4 cps to a low of approximately .5 cps.

The significance of all this is that the *higher* the cps produced, the *less control* we have over our brain systems because *less energy* is *available* to stimulate and charge our body cells. The fact that at the Alpha level up to 120 mv (micro volts) of electricity is produced, as compared to only 8 to 12 mv produced at the normal Beta level, thoughts and ideas impressed upon the brain at the higher voltage will have a greater impact than those produced at a lower voltage. Because of the higher voltage produced at the lower wave frequencies, it should become understandable why one can go into Alpha and come out so refreshed in a matter of minutes: the higher voltage literally "recharges" the body cells!

From all that has been said of Alpha, I hope you don't take it mean it is a panacea for making your life better, because, in itself, it is neither essential or a causative factor in that respect. What good or bad that becomes a part of your life is strictly of your own doing ...with or without Alpha. As a means to assist you in utilizing your full potential, however, Alpha control is both essential and causative. And used properly, there is no limit to what you can do or accomplish through the use of it. Now let's turn to those bad habits you'd probably like to rid yourself of.

WHAT HABIT CAN DO, IT CAN UNDO

Can you imagine what it would be like to awaken each morning and have to learn ...all over again... how to get out of bed, how to walk to the bathroom, how to get dressed, how to eat breakfast, how to brush your teeth, how to drive to work and so on? If there's such a thing as an impossibility, this would be it. But, as we all know, such is not the case in the human experience because we have a brain system, and once it has experienced something, the memory of it is never lost. Fortunately, because of this, it is possible to take the memory of one experience, add it to another, and in turn add them to still other experiences until a "pattern" of success is sufficiently formed enough to instruct the system in how to carry-out certain specific acts, such as walking, driving a car, employing the use of the multiplication tables, and so on. Once these "patterns" have been shaped and formed in the memory, all of the trials and tribulations that go into making them up are no longer necessary because the pattern, itself, becomes the prominent experience and in turn take the place of all the separate complexities which make it up. Such is the basis for forming any habit ...good or bad.

A pattern of habit is formed in three steps: *motivation, experience* and *repetition*. The habit of smoking, for instance, is acquired in the following way: Someone offers you a cigarette for the first time. If you accept it and smoke it, it is because you have the desire and are thereby *motivated* to do so. Once you have smoked it, you have experienced it. If the motivating desire has been justified by the *experience*, the act will undoubtedly be *repeated* again in the future. If it is repeated, and it is done at frequent intervals, it is on its way to becoming a habit, but not necessarily a habit in the sense that it fulfills the desire to smoke; it becomes, rather, a habit stemming from a *conditioned-reflex* action; a reaction to a condition that has nothing to do with a pleasurable experience, but rather to a condition brought about by a number of factors which were present while the habit was being formed as revealed in Pavlov's classic experiment with dogs.

In this particular experiment, Pavlov rang a bell every time a dog was given food. After repeating this act a number of times, it wasn't long before the dog's flow of saliva became as thoroughly associated with the ringing bell as it was with the sight of food. Before long, all Pavlov had to do was ring the bell in place of setting food out, and the dog would salivate ...a conditioned-reflex action.

And so it seems to be the case with the habit of smoking for most people: nervousness and tension, like a ringing bell, were no doubt present while the habit of smoking (for pleasure?) was being formed. Once the association of such a condition became established in the memory, any suggestion of nervousness and tension experienced by the mind automatically triggered (a conditioned-reflex action) a desire to smoke.

In attempting to break people of the habit of smoking, some anti-smoking centers have logically assumed that the trend can be broken by utilizing the same conditioned-reflex actions as discovered by Pavlov, only in reverse, in that each time a person reaches for a cigarette they should receive a shock, be given a pill or something to establish a new condition to discourage their desire to smoke. The logic is good, of course, but it's hardly effective over the long run because of the psychological factors involved. Unfortunately this same approach has been tried in treating alcoholics as well. In most cases the results in both instances are temporary at best for most people, primarily because, as seems to be the accepted procedure in treating any kind of social ill in this country, the tendency is to treat the *effects* rather than the *cause*.

It is true, in cases of excessive smoking and drinking, conditions of nervousness, tension, etc., they can be considered as causative agents, but certainly not the initial cause. What is the *cause* of nervousness and tension? Therein lies the answer, and only after treating "it" can an effective result be obtained. Sure, you can shock people and make them sick very time they light-up or take a drink, and possibly you can break them of the habit temporarily, but in doing so, if you don't treat the initial cause of the problem directly, the so-called cure could wind-up causing more of a problem than the habit you're trying to overcome ...like eliminating the habit of smoking in exchange for a case of ulcers or psoriases.

It must be remembered that whatsoever people think or do ...good or bad... they do so because of the causative action brought about by what they've *experienced in the past*. And in the case of trying to eliminate an undesirable effect, the only way it can be accomplished without causing still further undesirable effects is to remove, displace, or overcome the initial causative experience behind it. A desire to smoke, being motivated to smoke, smoking because of a built-in conditioned-reflex action; such things are brain-oriented. And whether their origin be psychological or physiological in nature, like all matters of the brain, they can be purposely controlled (eliminated or reinforced) by proper programming.

As before, in order to program effectively, you must define a plan. In the case of breaking or overcoming any undesirable habit, your plan should include the following: First, write a brief statement detailing all the draw-backs pertaining to the habit, including an analysis of the reasons why you think you do it, i.e., tension, insecurity, frustration, peer pressure, etc. Next, write a statement covering all the benefits you expect to gain once the habit is eliminated from your life. Now follow this up with a statement of affirmation; keeping in mind that it should be positive and stated in the present tense. For example, in the case of smoking, I would suggest an affirmation along this line: "*I no longer smoke because I am free of all tension, frustration and anxiety!*" In the case of excessive drinking, just substitute it for smoking. Like or similar phrasing can also be used for any other undesirable habit which is not a necessary part of the human experience i.e., drug abuse, nail-biting, bed wetting, etc.

It should be noted, that in the affirmation "I no longer ...!" that the brain is not only being instructed to inhibit your desire to smoke, it is also receiving instructions to eliminate the determined cause behind it. In the future when someone offers you a cigarette, not only will you not have the desire to smoke for satisfaction, you won't have the desire to smoke out of necessity, either. Equally important, in the course of programming-out both types of desires, the chances of some hidden factor surfacing in the future which could cause you psychological or physiological problems later on is practically nil.

Once you have your habit reduced to the appropriate affirmation and committed it to memory, deal with it as you would with any other objective you have a desire to achieve; include it in your daily programming; give it time to nurture, and before you know it the change will begin to become a part of your life just as you want it to be!

As the success of one slight change, added to another becomes a part of your daily experiences, it will further reinforce what you are programming until a point is reached that you have formed the habit of being free of tension with no desire to smoke, drink, or whatever, because *what one habit can do, another habit can undo.*

WINNING IS A HABIT, AND SO IS LOSING

Maybe you would like to become a better sales person, actor, develop a better tennis stroke or golf swing, become better at anything that involves motivation, experience and repetition ...which accounts for at least 95% of what we do. If you happen to be a mediocre sales person at the moment, you are because you have formed the *habit* of being mediocre; mediocre, in that you have mediocre motivation, you have had mediocre experiences and you've allowed them to be repeated far too often. Hence, you're mediocre because you have formed the habit of being such. And as long as you continue to repeat the sales experiences considered to be mediocre, the habit of being mediocre is going to stay with you until you over-come it.

It's a funny thing about success, failure, and mediocrity: people don't just happen to become successful one day, fail the next and then settle down at being mediocre. Aside from temporary set-backs or surges of prosperity, people, generally, seek a level they are habitually comfortable with ...in accordance with their "Self-concept setting." If they are comfortable with success, they develop or instill the habit of being such. The same is true of people who are failures ...and, of course, those who are mediocre.

In that habits are initiated by motivation or desire, you're probably wondering why anyone would find comfort in being less than a success. It is simply because without *deeds, motivation and desire* one can accomplish very little. For example, if a mediocre actor desires to become a star but does nothing constructive about it, what then is going to make him a star ...solely the desire to be one? Even if given a starring role, lacking the ability to perform like a star, he will bomb-out as a star and fall back to the level of acting ability he is the most comfortable with ...mediocre.

Anyone desiring to become something they are not, must experience what they are not, first. As Reverend Ike, a fireball radio/TV pastor out of New York City, says: "You'll get to where you're going much faster if you look like you have already been there." In all cases such happenings can only be experienced in the Conscious first. Repeated enough times it becomes prominent in memory, leading to the experience becoming a habit. As the habit takes form in memory, it will bring about a comparable change in one's behavioral actions. As one's behavior begins to change, so will the effect of it become manifest in one's daily experiences. If it's a desire to become a top sales person, one must gather all the data one can on what makes a top sales person, and then program one's self accordingly. If it's to be the top of anything, the same procedure is called for; you must first ascertain exactly what characteristics and attributes are employed by those who are already at the top. Once discovered, try to fit them to your particular needs and then program them into your memory.

Consider what Johnny Miller, top professional golfer back in the 70s, had to say about such matters: "I'm very observant when it comes to the mechanics (of the golf swing). I love to watch people. I know what kinds of clubs most everybody on tour plays and what they do with their swing. The only way you're going to learn is by observing. When I see a great driver I try to observe exactly what he does different to be so good.

"And I've learned from talking. If I see something interesting I talk to the player about it. Or I mark it down or I analyze it or take pictures and analyze those.

"That's more interesting than going out and beating a lot of balls. I feel I can improve my swing by sitting home and just thinking about what I do. I can correct myself without even hitting a golf ball, and I do it a lot.

"I keep charts and records. I come up with key thoughts for my swing. I write them down. Otherwise I forget what I'm doing when I'm playing well."

Miller feels it is necessary to use mental imagery to train his system. "Before the shot," adds Miller, "I visualize the flight of the ball and the type of swing I want to use ...how the balls feels when it hits the clubface ...how it flies ...how it lands on the green ...this is programming your subconscious ...programming the computer. Then all I've got to do is pick the club, get over the ball and ...! I let my subconscious take over and it will hit the shot for me. That's why it's so important to see yourself on videotape or movies or in a mirror, because if you don't have an exact idea of what your swing looks like you won't communicate with your subconscious.

"Of course you must program a success. You must visualize the shot going on the green, the putt dropping in the hole. Don't program any bad shots.

"Your execution should be the same every time ...if you change, it fouls-up your muscle memory. The more programmed you are, the more automatic you become, the better you play."

So were the thoughts of Johnny Miller back in the 70's. You should have seen him in 1994; he was fantastic. After a long lay-off and eight or nine years with NBC serving as golf commentator, his grown-up kids talked him into playing in the Pebble Beach AT&T classic because he seemed to have overcome the putting "yips" ...the reason, by his own admission, he dropped out of golf for the years he did. Well, I'm not so sure he was completely cured, but he hung in there; competing with the best of the best. Miller beat 'em all! He beat them because all those years of programming himself to make a habit of success was still with him.

There are lots of Johnny Millers in the world today, and they don't all play golf either. There are "Johnny Miller" salesmen, actors, basketball players, bus drivers, musicians, clergymen, teachers, doctors, lawyers, housewives, stockbrokers, you name it; all have something in common: they've made a habit ...knowingly or otherwise... of being successful at what they do. Success didn't just happen to fall in their lap, either. Once motivated, they consciously or unconsciously programmed themselves toward success by learning from those who were. They probably learned by observation, discussion and analysis. Once learned, the experiences were probably written down, or well noted, and reduced to key thoughts (affirmations). Once programmed, their thoughts and action became automatic. Once their thoughts and actions became an automatic experience in their lives, they started "playing their game" better than most of the other players. Need I say more? Winning is mostly habit. So is losing.

LAST WORD ON HABITS

We'll now turn to those other bad habits you should and want to get rid of. These habits, unlike those just discussed, are not brought about by motivation and experience; they are, rather, habits that have "snuk" into your life through the proverbial "back door."

As said before, in order to *maintain* constructive concepts in your memory it is necessary that you not only continually reinforce experiences of how you want things to be, but that you should *consciously oppose* anything which is questionable as it pertains to your best interests as well. Let's begin with the "I can't!" syndrome.

As you know, all conscious and unconscious motivated expressions are real happening experiences to your memory. And because they are, they in turn automatically become a permanent part of it, meaning of course, they affect your thoughts and actions accordingly.

The only reason people "can't" do something is because they have allowed themselves to think they "can't." And the only reason they think they "can't" is because their memory contains a prominence of such data indicating it to be so.

Without giving it the slightest thought, most of us too often think and say adverse things we really don't mean, and without realizing it they consequently affect us in adverse ways. For instance, when you think, feel, speak the words "I can't find it!" or "I can't" make this thing work," more than likely you really can! The fact that you have impressed your memory with such information, and the fact that your brain carries out its function in accordance solely with the information made available to it, it has no other choice because it's instructions *compel* it to keep you from doing it. This, of course, is self-defeating and leads to a lot of unnecessary frustration on your part. It is suggested, therefore, in that the word "can't" is about as essential to a positive mental attitude as teats are to a boar, that the word "can't" be completely eliminated from your vocabulary and substituted with the more suitable, "I am unable at the moment to..." The logic of this is simple: The fact is, potentially, you can do anything you desire, and the more you can instill this fact upon your memory the more you're going to experience the results of it happening. Each time you impress your memory with the experience that you "can't" however ...no matter the innocence of the intent... it has the affect of eroding away and negating the fact that you "can."

"Can't," as commonly used, conveys the impression of finality. "Unable," on the other hand, leaves the door open; it suggests that the condition is only temporary. So do your thinking, feeling and voicing on a "temporary" basis, and you're more apt to find yourself doing things you thought you never could before. For instance, if you find you are unable to attend a party, reply that you are "unable." If you think you're unable to find something or make it work, don't envision that you "can't." Instead, think in terms that the matter will be resolved shortly, which it will if you infer to your memory that it will.

Once you become aware of the use of "can't" in your own memory, you will surely become aware of others using it as well. To further displace its prominence in your memory, it is suggested that you make a practice of overcoming the word whenever it comes to mind by mentally saying to yourself **"Cancel, Cancel!"** It is further suggested that you do this for all words implying negative connotations: words like "cannot," "never," "impossible," etc. You'll be surprised how your concepts will begin to change once you begin eliminating such negativisms from your memory files.

As for the "good luck, bad luck" syndrome, that is another matter. "Luck" is a term that has probably been around since the beginning of humankind. Depending upon its prefix (good or bad), it, by far has more-than-likely had the greatest single impact upon the lives of people world-wide than any other words known to man. Believing they had luck on their side, countless people have achieved success far beyond their dreams, just as countless others, believing luck was working against them, have experienced failure to the same degree.

What is it about luck anyway? Does it consist of two aspects, i.e., one working for you and the other against you? Is it something which can be wooed and won? Or is it something allusive like a butterfly ...never knowing what the results will be if and when it touches you? Whatever it is, it must be something of substance, because every language known to man makes reference to it in some form or another.

Suppose we consider it in the light of what you have so far learned about yourself. Could it be that the inference of "luck" is an expression which has been passed down through the ages to describe a happening or condition that exists but lacks an apparent or explainable cause? I believe it is. I think it is an ignorance-realized revelation of the possibilities made possible by a brain unconsciously attuned to the Medium. In other words, without knowing it, those who have experienced good as-well-as bad luck did not experience the effects of something referred to as luck, but rather the effects produced as a result of their own brain impressing the Medium with causative thoughts of how they wanted things to be. For those who believe they are unlucky, they generally "are" because, according to their faith that they are unlucky, it is given unto them. It is precisely the same for those who believe they are lucky ...it is given unto them in accordance with their faith that they are lucky.

To me, the effects of luck and superstition are essentially the same; both rely upon faith. If a person breaks a mirror, for instance, and entertains the idea that he/she is going to have seven years of bad luck, it's more than likely they will; not because "bad luck" is set upon them, but because they choose to believe (having faith) that such a so-called force will act upon them. And what makes it so believable, is that with such a belief held in their memory, the first experience of adversity (more than likely unrelated) to come along, it is immediately associated with the breaking of the mirror. This in turn reinforces the belief that "luck" is working against them just that much more.

I have played golf with several chaps over the years who will only play with a certain numbered ball. They miss short putts with it, they knock it out of bounds, into hazards and trees, and so on. Yet they think it's their "lucky" ball. Interestingly enough, in switching to another numbered ball, they usually play worse. This, of course, is all the evidence they need to substantiate the fact in their memory that one numbered ball is "luckier" than another ...never realizing, of course, that it is not the fact that one numbered ball is luckier than another, but rather that believing it to be so, so it is, insofar as their memory is concerned. And that is what's so significant about the concept of luck as it is used here. It exemplifies everything we have discussed so far: that what a person is and the conditions he/she finds a part of their life, is directly related to the thoughts they choose and encourage. And whether they choose to call it luck, superstition, the work of the Gods, Goddesses, or whatever, it all amounts to the same thing: that what a person chooses to believe, so it will be for that person. It can be no other way!

The brain is a goal-seeking learning machine capable of achieving the highest of highs as well as the lowest of lows. It makes no difference to your brain which it is, up or down. It's objective is always the same: that it carry out its function in strict accordance *with the information made available to it.* So long as you choose to believe a black cat walking across your path is going to bring you bad luck, so it will be in your experiences. This is true of anything you choose to believe ...providing, of course, you truly believe it. And that's where luck gets its allusive reputation.

Often times we confuse belief with that of hope. Hoping this to be our lucky day does not always produce the results we desire. Whereas, believing with assurance that this "is" our lucky day, it more than often turns out that way.

My only objection to the use of the word luck is the inference it suggests. In wishing a person good luck, although your intentions may be admirable, the inference is that you may *hope* some force of unexplainable origin will look kindly upon them. To me, that's equivalent of whistling in the dark. And for the person intended, to think that your wishing them good luck is going to affect their future happenings, that too, is like a whistle in the dark. If you really wish the best for someone, tell them: "I wish you well!" In doing so, place your faith in the fact that you can effect the future happenings in their life by mentally picturing it taking place in your own brain as you want it to be for them. For them, if they are aware of your intentions, then they have something worthwhile going for them: two brains instead of one impressing the Medium with definitive thoughts ..it produces a greater effect than the impressions made by one brain working alone.

Yes, luck is something all right, and there's no denying it. But it's not allusive. And it's not unexplainable. Luck is a misconceived concept of the effects produced by faith, the most formidable force known to man because it has the backing of ultimate Truth and Law behind it. Faith by itself, is neither good or bad, it is only what you choose to make of it.

Lastly there is the "typical of" syndrome. Years ago when I was selling Real Estate, it was not unusual to find one's-self faced with unduly long dry spells when no sales were made. The "word" in the office was, that this was "typical of the business." And so it was to those of us who subscribed to such thinking. But to those who didn't, they were making deals in spite of it. For one who's been-there done-that it's easy to understand why: those making the sales were the ones who refused to buy the concept that "it was typical of the business." That, of course, is the difference between a Real Estate "salesman" and a Real Estate "person." The people who are consistent in making sales in any business are those who consciously oppose the adverse aspects of their surroundings from quietly establishing a foothold in their memory. By thinking only of how they want things to be they inadvertently deny the suggestive experiences of their surroundings to influence their system. Denied a role of recognition, *nothing can affect the system.* And when unable to affect the system it cannot become a manifest condition because insofar as the memory is concerned, it does not exist.

What I found to be true in real estate is true in all business: that selling *is* an up and down situation, but only to those who allow themselves to believe that it is. Even in the business of professional golf this is true: The general feeling or "word" on the tour is, that if you get out in front of the pack too early, the pressure in the closing round is going to get to you, causing you to fold in the stretch. And so it is to those who choose to accept what is "typical of the business." But to those who consciously oppose such influencing suggestions, they often run away with all the marbles leaving the others wondering why.

Again, the cause of all adversity can only be found in the memory files of the brain system. Denied a foothold by overcoming it with contrary data, its effectiveness is lost, and the reality of it no longer exists in memory.

Summary

Looking back on what we've covered so far, it is my hope that together we've eliminated much of the ignorance you may have had in the past about yourself, your surroundings and the rest of humankind; that you now view everything with a different and better informed perspective. Hopefully that new perspective includes a greater appreciation for *who* you truly are as one of Nature's finest accomplishments, and that you have a better understanding of *why* you are what you are today and *what* you can do to change and start making things happen in your life as you want them to be. Equally important, I hope your new perspective has made it clear to you that all of humankind are essentially the same ...as is an aborigine from Australia the same as a Thomas Jefferson from America... but at the same time, different ...the difference not being a lack of potential and capability to equal or surpass the accomplishments of anyone else in this world, but rather a difference based solely upon what each has personally experienced from his or her respective surroundings in the past.

Okay. There should be no doubt in your brain where your true potential and capability lies. You should know exactly why you are the person you are today, and you should also know what you can do to change it and how. Now it's up to you. Only you can make thing happen in your life as you want them to be.

No more can you blame your failures on circumstances and what others do. No more can you hide behind the cloak of being brought up in the wrong neighborhood, coming from a broken home, being short-changed on your education, never getting an opportunity, or anything else. Yes, such things had a lot to do with why you are what you are today, but not for what you can become tomorrow. They no longer apply, because you can negate or displace your past experiences with those of your own choosing today.

Simple put, you have no excuse for falling short of your dreams because you now know how to make things happen in your life just as you want them to be. From now on it's your show. As you choose to think, so it will be for you. It can be no other way!

In bringing this to an end, I would like to leave you with a simple but sage bit of advice. Remember it well: If *you* don't control your mind, *somebody else will!* ...which just happens to be the underlying message I'll be covering in my next book. In the meantime I would like to leave you with this bit of wisdom by James Allen from his book, As a Man Thinketh: "Act is the blossom of thought, and joy and suffering are its fruits; thus does a man harvest the sweet and bitter fruits of his own husbandry."

MY GUARANTEE

As is the case with any of my publications, if you, for any reason, feel this book has not helped you in your endeavor to be *the best you can become* to the degree that satisfies you, you may, at any time, return the book accompanied by the shipping label or sales receipt to me, personally, and I will refund your purchase price.

Also, should you wish to make any comments, suggestions, or if you find you're having difficulty carrying-out the instructions in this book and you wish to have them explained, please feel free to write or call me. I will be pleased to hear from you and will respond accordingly.

I wish you well! Enjoy the journey!

Dudley Wolford
P.O. Box 1780
Sisters, OR 97759
(541) 549-2014